HELPING CHILDREN WRITE

HELPING CHILDREN WRITE

A Thinking Together About Children's Creative Writing

MAUREE APPLEGATE

Rural Department, State Teachers College,
La Crosse, Wisconsin

INTERNATIONAL TEXTBOOK COMPANY
SCRANTON, PENNSYLVANIA

48272

THE HADDON CRAFTSMEN, INC.
SCRANTON, PENNSYLVANIA

Acknowledgements

The author wishes to thank these children for their contribution to this book:

From Neenah, Wisconsin

Clara Albert, Gr. 7
Dallas Anderson, Gr. 7
Dick Baer, Gr. 7
Chester Bell, Gr. 8
Eric Bergstrom, Gr. 5
Gene Brooks, Gr. 8
Carol Buchanan, Gr. 6
Joyce Bunker, Gr. 4
Robert Campbell, Gr. 7
Kay Carlson, Gr. 2
Florence Christian, Gr. 5
Marjorie Clark, Gr. 4
Robert Ducklow, Gr. 7
Edward Faulks, Gr. 5
Douglas Freund, Gr. 1
Barbara Fuszard, Gr. 7
Gale Graff, Gr. 7
Marilyn Eckstein, Gr. 6
Nancy Haley, Gr. 2
Wayne Halverson, Gr. 5
Carleton Hoppe, Gr. 5
Eric Johnson, Gr. 7
John Kalfass, Gr. 4
Ralph Komps, Gr. 4
Betty Kimberley, Gr. 1
Charles Knaak, Gr. 6
Letty Koch, Gr. 6

Courtney Kohr, Gr. 4
Joanne Labb, Gr. 7
Robert Larson, Gr. 6
Kirk Lawson, Gr. 7
Jane Lechming, Gr. 4
Sally Madsen, Gr. 4
Carol Meartz, Gr. 5
Jacqueline Miller, Gr. 5
Merrill Miller, Gr. 6
Richard Neller, Gr. 7
Dick Neubauer, Gr. 2
Shirley Parker, Gr. 2
Mary Peterson, Gr. 6
Jerry Pues, Sr. Kindergarten
Ruth Pyatt, Gr. 1
Beverly Rawson, Gr. 1
Eddie Rodden, Gr. 5
Bob Schultz, Gr. 8
Connie Smith, Gr. 6
James Smith, Gr. 5
Joan Smith, Gr. 6
Marlene Spoo, Gr. 4
Brian Stompe, Gr. 4
Kay Thompson, Jr. Kindergarten
Peter Thomsen, Gr. 4
Tom Thomsen, Gr. 7
David Verhagen, Gr. 4

Those who wrote articles for the school newspaper, Gr. 2, McKinley School:

Jean, Herbert, Ronald, Edward, Sandra, Leah, Carl, Deboyd, Earl, Reuben, Ellen, Edythe, Norma, Patsy, and Marshall.

Those who wrote the Athenian News, p. 165-166:

Joan Hagen, Joyce Redlin and three children who wrote unsigned articles.

Those who wrote the four letters on p. 116-117:

Sally, Dorothy, Sharon, and Polly.

v

Those who wrote the autobiographical sketches (Gr. 5) Washington School.

Those who wrote these class poems:

Kimberly—Gr. 6
Lincoln School—Gr. 1
Roosevelt School—Gr. 1
Washington School—Gr. 1

Those who wrote the story on p. 55

(No names) Washington School Senior Kindergarten.

From Elm Grove State Graded School, La Crosse County, Wisconsin

Joyce Ciana, Gr. 5
Phyllis Culbert, Gr. 6
Dale Hendrecks, Gr. 6
Phyllis Kately, Gr. 7
Eunice Kingelman, Gr. 6
Lorraine Kummel, Gr. 6
Brice Nelson, Gr. 4
Valerie Peart, Gr. 5

The children who wrote these poems:

Group poem, Gr. 5-8
Class poems, Gr. 5
Class poems, Gr. 6

Those who wrote for the Elm Grove Broadcaster:

Betty Jean Kately
Dale Hendren
Paula Beyer

From Viroqua, Wisconsin

Ann Louise Allness

From Rock County, Wisconsin

Dean Bickle, Gr. 7, Red Brick School
Rebecca Carver, Gr. 6
Boyd Dillree, Tupper School
Ray Dummell, Gr. 6, North Milton School
Betty Ruth Fisher, Gr. 8, Austin School
Shirley Green, Gr. 6, Washburn School
Donald Jones, Gr. 4, Washburn School
John Kaufman, Gr. 5, Newville School
Shirley Klug, Gr. 4, North Milton School
Donald ————— (A school in Fulton Twp.)
Helen Smith, Gr. 6, Otter Creek School
Marlene Troon, Gr. 3, Paul School
Shirley Troon, Gr. 4, Red Brick School

The children who wrote the letters:
    (No name), Shirley Green, Donald Jones

From Jefferson County, Wisconsin
    Donald Riebe, Grade 1, Stony Brook School

From Monroe County, Wisconsin
    Betty Gerwig, Grade 8

From Galesville, Wisconsin
    Kathryn Beadle, Gr. 3

From Shawano, Wisconsin
    Darwin Born, Gr. 8

From Appleton, Wisconsin, publishers of Cheery Chatter, Gr. 6, Roosevelt
    Jr. High School: Fredrick Zwicker, Helen Rehbein, Mary Cooper, Bar-
    bara Bailey, Sally Wilkinson, Paul Lewis, and Donna Christian.

From the Training School at Stevens Point
    Editors and reporters of the Sixth Grade Press; Marion Klein, Lois
    Nelson, Karen Mortenson, Jean Eagleberger.

The author and the International Textbook Company wish to
thank:

Harcourt, Brace and Company, Inc. for permission to print one of Carl
    Sandburg's "Definitions of Poetry" and for permission to use two
    lines from Louis Untermeyer's "Peter Putter."

The Macmillan Company for permission to quote twice from Vachel
    Lindsay's "The Congo and Other Poems."

Scott, Foresman and Company for permission to use two dictionary games
    from their publication "Middle-Grade Activities."

The Milwaukee Journal, a newspaper of Milwaukee, Wisconsin, for
    permission to reprint two local news items.

Wide World Photos, Inc. for permission to reprint two Associated-Press
    news items.

Foreword

"If I COULD turn Sammy Sloan's mind inside out, I swear I'd find Roman stripes inside instead of gray matter. That kid has more streaks than Christmas Candy."

The principal heard Miss M.'s clear voice down the deserted school corridor, followed by a general burst of laughter.

It was half-past four and she was sitting at her desk looking at a grubby piece of paper with a misspelled scrawl of verse across it. She could just make out the "Sammy" at the end.

The principal read the verse again and again. She *was* holding Sammy Sloan's mind inside out in her hand. Miss M. was right, Sammy had a rainbow inside.

Contents

Chapter I

Treasures

Little boy's pockets hold amazing things—

Fishworms, apple cores, a mess of strings—

*But this treasure is nothing to the wealth
  one finds*

In little boys' hearts and in little boys' minds.

Chapter I

Treasures

O HELP CHILDREN, we must know children. It is hard to understand people who play-act much of the time. Children have learned that it is usually wiser not to be themselves before adults. They have tried it too many times with disappointment.

A child will no sooner turn out the pockets of his mind to one he does not trust than a shy little boy will turn out the treasures of his trousers pocket to a stranger. He has so many wonderings, questions, fears, and dreams, and so few adult friends with whom he can share them. This is why the elementary teacher is turning so eagerly to creative writing. It is another way of getting to know children.

The average teacher feels that she knows little about creative writing. She wants to go to summer school to learn how to teach it. Creativeness cannot be taught; it can only be released and guided. This, in essence, is the job of the teacher—to release inner power into productive outer channels. The world does not need more talented children; it needs to release and develop the talents latent in all children. This does not demand creative teachers trained in creative writing; it calls for receptive and understanding teachers.

Writing starts from ideas—and children are full of ideas. Creative ideas are those we believe in so strongly that they pound on the inner door to be released. It does not matter whether a teacher assigned the writing or we assigned it to ourselves; if we feel it, we can be taught to write it. Writing without feeling is anemic and bloodless, and the writer has no pride in it. Creative writing, then, is writing that pushes itself out of a bed of ideas. It may not be particularly original.

1

Only a few ideas are startlingly original. We may have sent our roots far to gather the material that went into our letter or report or story or poem; but it has gone through the magic plant of ourselves, and this synthesis we have achieved is ours. And because it is ours, we can learn to develop a pride in making it better; it is so much more fun to improve something that belongs to ourselves. Even the dull child is thrilled to write about his own interests. The modern school room, with its many areas of interest and its thought-producing activities, is a natural seed bed for creative writing. Never have school children been more filled with things to say. A teacher need not worry because she lacks ideas; boys and girls will often react better to teachers who are receptive than to those who are continually stimulating.

What does creative writing do for boys and girls other than to help them to express themselves better? (And, goodness knows, they need that.) For one thing it provides them with chimneys. Look around you at the happiest folks. They are those who have discovered chimneys to release their inner steam and pressure. For instance, Jim Black, in fifth grade is puzzled about something that has happened at home. If he can work off those questions in his mind by feeling free to write a story, he may be able to gain inside peace without an emotional explosion. He can drop the story into the story box without any of the children noticing. True, the same purpose can be accomplished if Jim paints, draws, or models his emotion out, or plays it out on the piano, or planes it away with the shavings of the table he is making. Any of these outlets can provide a chimney for a child's emotion. If his school has provided a varied creative program, it will be natural for Jim to choose the chimney best suited to him. He may want to choose writing because he can use it so quietly that no one will know what he is really thinking. Thinking things through with the fingers is infinitely better for an individual than brooding. Our way of life—while it offers much in the way of release—offers too little in the way of creative expression, which rests as it tires. Creative writing is one of many chimneys which schools can provide, with no further outlay of money.

Creative writing gives children something to be proud of. I have seen apparently colorless personalities blossom under the warm sun of approval when their poems or stories were read to the class or were published in the class story book. I have seen these same children gain in confidence and poise, and I have noticed that for the first time they had a sense of pride in themselves as human beings. Pride is the starch which puts a bit of stiffening into limp folks whom the washing machine of life has subjected to rough treatment. A teacher who judges the efficacy of creative writing by what it has done to the writer will use entirely different standards for judging the writing than will the teacher who is engrossed with the writing as an end in itself.

Creative writing helps children to discover their own capabilities. The few gifted writers in your room will write whether given a chance to write or not. The majority of children will not be interested in writing unless you, their teacher, are interested. It would be the same if your chief interest were Timbuktu or spiders or Abraham Lincoln. Children will follow any pied piper who calls to them with a beckoning tune. They love to pretend to be this or that anything but themselves—and many of them will write better about a "pretend" than a "real." By degrees, one child after another in your room will find out that writing is fun—real fun. There are many who might never have discovered this without your assistance.

If you have no particular feeling for words as a medium of expression or if your deepest thoughts flatten out on paper, can you still help children to write? This book and the books listed in the bibliography in the last chapter will help you to answer that question. *Helping Children Write* is a primer lesson; a first step in helping you to get a few standards for yourself and to get a few practical ways of starting a creative program. This book might, after the fashion of manuals, be entitled, *First Steps in Helping Children to Write Creatively*. After it will come broader, deeper books and articles to help you to acquire finesse. But first you must learn to believe in yourself, to believe in what writing can do for children and for you, and to learn some simple rules of the writing game.

You will make a grave mistake if you try to follow exactly the ideas suggested here—as creativeness follows no paths. However, it has acquired a few helpful techniques. Music needs voice exercises in one form or another, and drawing must adhere to the rules of perspective and proportion; but writing has too often been taught by the simple method of pushing the young writers off into a void and saying, "Write a poem for English." A few children learn to use their wings in this fashion, and a few call upon friends and relatives for help; but infinitely more children develop a distaste for writing.

The children's writing found in these pages was not—except in a few cases—done by talented children in exclusive neighborhoods. For the most part, it was written by average children with little flair for writing. But average children—and most children are average—have things to say if anyone cares to listen, and they can be taught to say them more clearly and in a better way. Often the more sensitive the child, the less articulate he is and the more he is in need of a medium of expression that is a little more private than talking.

Some of the children's writing included here is not of high quality. You will get more bad writing than good when seeking self-expression in children. Teachers of creative writing are more interested in what writing does for children than in what children write. They are more interested in individual growth than in comparative products. If the end product is the goal of writing, pattern work will produce a better product, but it will not change children. The pattern teacher spends her time tying leaves on dead trees; the teacher of creative writing creates a climate where leaves can grow naturally. If and when the growth comes, she can do something about it. This growth and what to do about it are the concern of this book.

How will you know good writing when you see it? Good writing is a process of growth, just as taste is a process of growth. Children and most adults go through stages of appreciation of good writing. Many adults get no further than the jingle stage of verse and the pulp-magazine stage of prose. Your job is to get children to want to grow in their literary tastes, and it is necessary for you to furnish experiences which will allow for that growth. In the meantime, you will want to improve your own literary tastes in the same way. Soon you will not be content with poetry that answers questions, and you will find out that only the poem that leaves a questioning in your mind is real poetry. Instead of being content with such ordinary verse as that which introduces each chapter of this book, you will read *The Cairn*, by Edna St. Vincent Millay, and every day, as the poem writes itself deeper into your heart, you will try to answer the question, "What is vital in this business of teaching?"

As you read, you might try your hand at writing. If you feel like telling your principal just what you think of him, write it; then quietly throw the paper into the furnace. You will find words a fascinating medium of expression. A sentence can be as full of color as a tempera painting, and as moving as organ music; it can shout as loudly as an intermediate child on the playground, or can whisper as softly as a shy first grader. While you are helping children to write, there is a secret satisfaction in finding out what you can do with words. In the meanwhile, read a little every day from a really good book. Read prose and poetry aloud to yourself, until the beauty of the spoken word casts its spell upon you. Read aloud to your children. Choose books a level or two above what children can read for themselves. Don't make the mistake of talking much about the book. Great stories need no artificial respiration to make them alive to others. They need merely to be read; first together, later alone.

From reading to writing is a natural step. Reading and writing have always lived next door to each other, but few people have found the hole in the hedge between them. It is through wide reading that one learns to write; and it is through writing that one learns the fine points of reading.

Can you teach children to write creatively? Only the pattern teacher is foolish enough to think that she can. But you can help children to release the creativity within them that seeks expression. If you prove yourself a friend to children, and they find you worthy, they will share with you the treasures of their hearts.

Chapter II

Sprouts of Wings

My little black pony flies over the ground—

He can gallop and cantor and trot.

He has all of the things—even sprouts of wings—

That Pegasus has got.

Chapter II

Sprouts of Wings

POETRY is the language of childhood. This is because children and poets are discoverers—discoverers of new worlds and new ideas. To a poet each discovery is as fresh and as new as if no one in the world had ever made it before. When he tells of his discovery, he uses a fresh way of expressing what he has seen. He must   he is telling about what to him is a new thing.

It is as though you had gone out into your back yard just now (I hope you have one; if you haven't, you can pretend) and found there a queer animal like none you had ever seen or heard of before, even in a Disney cartoon. You see this strange creature and run back to tell your family about it. What do you say? You might not realize it, but your description of the animal would be either in terms of some animal you already know or in terms coined to fit the new experience. This happens to a poet and to a child every day. That is why they describe one thing in terms of another. That is why they coin new words.

A baby, having already experienced the sensation of light, one night discovers the moon; and holding out his hands toward his discovery says, "Piece of light!" He must use words that he knows to make his discovery intelligible to you. Later on this same baby may, as I heard one do, tell you solemnly that one light switch turns on the light and the other turns on the dark. Children and poets speak the same language.

Let us suppose that this baby never gets over being a poet—that the exigencies of living do not fit his soul with myopic glasses. He will keep right on discovering the moon.

But now his experiences will have enlarged. He will have so
many ways to tell us of his discovery. The moon may now be
"the North Wind's cooky"[1] or

> "The Moon? It is a griffin's egg,
> Hatching tomorrow night."[2]

Poets never quit being children, but unfortunately children too often quit being poets.

Read this talking poem I heard a four-year-old say one
day to her mother as they rode along in the car:

> "Daddy looks so funny when he smiles;
> He looks just like the moon.
> Mommy, does the moon smile?
> Where is the moon in the wintertime?
> I bet he's sound asleep."

Notice the natural poetry of the speech of this junior
kindergarten youngster. She was talking to her group at
school:

> "This morning when I opened my closet door,
> My shoes were cuddling each other with their shoe-strings.   1
> I did not spank them.
> I let them do what they wanted to do."

Children are born poets, but they can easily become verse-
makers. Shall we stop here and clear up the difference between a poet and a verse maker? I can explain only through
the use of an analogy.

When you were little, you swayed to the rhythm of
music—unconsciously, of course, but with more or less perfect
timing. Then you were a poet. Later, at the age of ten or
twelve, you went to a dancing school and learned how to
count your steps. You were self-conscious and a little awk-

---

[1] From Vachel Lindsay: *The Congo and Other Poems.* Copyright, 1914, by
The Macmillan Company and used with their permission.
[2] "Yet Gentle Will the Griffin Be"—ibid.

ward at first. Now you are beginning to be a verse-maker. One day, all of a sudden, you forgot about counting and about your feet and you really danced. Now you are both a verse-maker and a poet.

When children begin to translate the music of their souls into measured steps, they become verse-makers—but their first attempts are awkward and crude. Poets have to learn all over again to talk the way they talked naturally when they were children.

If they begin young enough to make verses, children make the transition naturally. Having no preconceived rules about rhythm and rhyme, or form or meter, children make up their own and the result pleases them. Their verses are apt to be jingles because they love to hear the sound of words brushing against each other. Many of their verses do not make sense to adults. This does not bother the verse-maker, young or old, because a poet and a child are natural egoists. When they have once eaten of the fruit of the tree of public opinion, they lose the private worlds in which they were kings and thus lose the honesty of true poets.

The formal school room gradually strips the blossoms of creative speech from the lips of children. Only the child with the marked talent for the picturesque still retains his original language. Year after year the speech of each becomes a little more the speech of all, until during the adolescent period it takes on an actual pattern. The door of creativity shuts fast and, for many, never opens again.

The wise kindergarten or primary teacher does not allow the door to begin to shut. She makes the writing of stories and poems something to look forward to. She writes down the stories and jingles her children tell to her, and puts them into a book for them to see. "Wait until you are in first grade," she promises, "then you can write all by yourself. You can write stories about what you think and see."

There is no more powerful incentive for learning to write than this. She praises a new way of describing the outdoor things the children bring into the school room. Picturesque speech becomes the desirable speech. Through daily use the door of creativeness swings freely on its hinges.

Many primary teachers, who get stories to grow naturally in their rooms, have no success with verse-making.

"To tell the truth," one bright young teacher confided to me, "I am afraid of children's verse. I don't know how to guide it. A few children come out with it naturally, but I wish more of my children were interested in verse-making. They so love to have me read poetry to them."

"Why don't you begin writing down their jingles?" I suggested. "That is where most teachers begin, and where all children start their verse-making."

A jingle is a puppy poem that seems to play with the sound of words but pays little attention to their meaning. Nursery rhymes are usually of this type. It doesn't matter what they mean, so long as the jingle of the rhyme and the bounce of the rhythm is a delight. Primary children often string together, one after the other, meaningless rhyming words and chuckle to themselves as they do it.

Such jingle-type poems as "The Three Foxes" by A. A. Milne[1] not only make use of natural rhyme but also make up rhyming words—a practice in which children have always delighted because they enjoy doing it themselves. You will have fun reading poetry to your school children and finding out which poems they enjoy.

Many children in high school, and even an occasional teacher, have never gone beyond the jingle, ear-tickling stage of poetry appreciation. They still believe that verse must

---

[1] Milne, A. A., *When We Were Very Young*. E. P. Dutton and Co., 1924, p. 38-40.

have a distinct rhyme and that the sense of the verse is secondary to the rhyme.

My classic example of this belief is an actual rhyme a sixth-grader wrote. To her, rhyme was paramount. She was writing, not because she had something to say but because she wanted to make a rhyme. Her verse follows:

> I went out to my grandfather's farm,
> And when I got there, he had broken his arm.
> I looked for the kitten,
> But she was a-sitten,
> So I thought I had better go home.

This child had almost a perfect sense of rhythm, but very little idea of what verse is.

A jingle is to the poetry world what a jolly dance is to our daily living. Jingles belong to that very important part of our lives which is devoted to recreation and fun.

Doggerel verse is not like a jingle. It pays more attention to meaning. It is sometimes "wise-cracking," timely verse—as useless tomorrow as yesterday's newspaper. It is often crude in style, and yet is sometimes howlingly funny. Adolescents in junior and senior high schools write doggerel about their classmates and their teachers. Doggerel is a stage of poetry writing. The true difference between it and the later stage of poetry is in its obviousness. It is easy to know what the writer of doggerel means. He tells you directly. On the other hand, no one but the poet who wrote a mature poem could ever tell you exactly what his poem means. You know what his poem means to you, but you can only guess what it meant to him. He may be using symbols to express his thoughts. This is the difference, too, between children and adults—directness of meaning.

The word "doggerel" is not a pretty word. It is better to apply the term *verse* or *rhyme* to children's attempts at poetry. There is something a little insulting in the word "doggerel," but such verse has a real place in the growing-up of a poet and efforts to write it should be encouraged. The lines of children's verse often "bulge" at the seams because what they have to say is more important to children than how they say it. I am glad that this is true. Form comes when the thought being expressed is important enough to the writer to be worked over and over.

Children's early verse is very revealing. There are many implications for teachers in this bit written by a sixth-grade pupil about report cards:

REPORT CARDS

Report cards are funny things.
When you get them
You wouldn't exactly like to sing.
Some are good
And some are very bad.
You should have seen the one a girl had.
It had red F's and D's.
If I had my way,
There would be no report cards—starting today.

From jingles, through doggerel and parody, with now and then four lines of breath-taking beauty, goes the child poet in the process of growing up. Some day he may be a real poet. If not, he will be a better person for having used his wings while he had them.

What is real poetry? I wish I knew. Carl Sandburg,[1] in his "Ten Definitions of Poetry," says that poetry is "the synthesis of hyacinths and biscuits." I have fun trying to make definitions of poetry. None of them ever satisfy me, and I tear them up and start all over again. Your pupils in junior high school also might like to try their hands at defining poetry.

---

[1] From *Good Morning, America* by Carl Sandburg. Copyright, 1928, by Carl Sandburg. Reprinted by permission of Harcourt, Brace and Company, Inc.

These are some of my attempts at trying to define poetry. Poetry is:

1. A song to which each one of us furnishes his own tune.
2. A mirror in which each of us sees himself.
3. A cloud woven together of a million raindrops of experience.
4. A riddle asked by a poet who isn't there to tell the answer.
5. Our most intimate thoughts dressed in masquerade; only those who know us will recognize them.
6. A garden of words sometimes planted in neat rows and sometimes growing wild.
7. A thought, an experience, a picture, a story or a song set into a design of words.

It is hard to define poetry; it is easier to describe it. Poetry is a different way of seeing something you may have looked at dozens of times and suddenly see for the first time. It is seeing the ordinary in an extraordinary way.

Explain to children that a poet never says to himself, "I must write a poem today." He has something to say and writes a poem to express his thought or feeling. You can tell by reading a child's verse whether his poem came from the inside out or he is just trying to write something.

It isn't necessary that a poem rhyme, but it must have rhythm flowing through it like the current in a creek or river. Rhymes are twin lines that are alike in sound but different in meaning.

Poetry is so often read badly, because it is read in a false, artificial way. It should be read just as you read prose. The sentences do not always stop at the rhyming words; they stop anywhere—even in the middle of a line. You will have no trouble if you read thoughts, rather than sentences. The punctuation will help you. Just pause when the thought pauses and stop when it stops. Poetry is made to be read aloud.

Poetry is really tuneless music; it has form and time. The form and timing of a poem match the idea it expresses. If the poem is sad, it is written in slow, solemn time. If it is joyful, it may have a lilting, skipping tempo. If it is quietly glad, it walks along slowly. If a poem is jerky, perhaps a word or a phrase should be added in order to make it go along smoothly. It is not necessary to scan children's verse. Read it aloud to feel the flow or break of the rhythm. Rhythm means the tempo of the poem. Note if it is walking, skipping, running, galloping, flying, dancing, or standing still.

There is one feeling more satisfying than coming upon a poem which says exactly what you have been feeling—that is to be able to write for yourself what you think and feel. You and I can help children to do this. It is a real service to be able to help even one child to establish communication between his inside world and the world outside.

How You Can Help Poetry to Grow in Your Own Room

Too many primary teachers, starting a creative program, work to get their children to say quaint things.

"I thought of the best idea for a poem on the way to school this morning," said one to me, "but I had the worst time getting my first-grade youngsters maneuvered into saying it." A creative program is not meant to require the maneuvering of ideas or the moving of a teacher's idea into a pupil's head. It is simply the creating of such an atmosphere in a school room that children's ideas may grow there naturally. It means planting seeds where no seeds were and making it possible for them to grow.

If you want your children to write poetry, you must become a poetry-reading teacher. This will do more than any other one thing that I know of to develop a taste for poetry in children. Start in kindergarten and read and read. Begin with only two or three poems at a time, but read often.

Notice the kind of poems that your group enjoys. Fit the poems to the group. Read just as you read prose—clearly and with feeling. Let your face help to read the poem. Don't hurry. If the children ask for a poem to be read again, read it again. Some poems, just like some people, need a little explanation before they are introduced. Make the explanation before you read, but do not do too much explaining. A poem means a different thing to each individual unless a grown-up spoils the effect by giving his or her interpretation.

The more fun you have in your poetry-reading time, the more your children will love poetry. They will enjoy, too, the warm, folksy atmosphere of appreciating things together.

Children like to hear poems other children have written. Most of all, they enjoy having their poems read aloud. Poetry was meant to be shared. Few children enjoy reading it silently.

There seems to be a direct correlation between the poetry-reading teacher and the poetry-writing class. No one knows exactly why. Perhaps it may happen in the way in which a girl learns to make a cake. She becomes so familiar with the process from watching the mother that one day she suddenly wants to try one for herself—so she does. It might be, too, that the teacher who reads poetry and enjoys it is a bit of a child at heart. Children are not afraid to trust her with their first wobbly attempts at verse-making.

If you want your children to write verse, you must take plenty of time to appreciate the little things that happen every day. Noticing the tree that has seemed to change color in the night; stopping to look at how the clouds are racing through the sky; noting how the shadows lengthen under the trees in the afternoon; watching together two lady robins gossip as they splash together in the bird bath—these are the little things that cause children to appreciate what is going on around them. While you are all interested together, one child is sure to make an observation that is sheer poetry or, at least, a "verse-starter."

Miss A...., a first grade teacher of my acquaintance, always takes time to enjoy chance happenings with her school children. One day the sun went suddenly behind a cloud during a reading class. The room grew as dark as twilight. Just as suddenly the sun shone brightly again.

"Miss A....", a child observed, "first it's bright and then it's night! Oh, I've made a poem! let's stop and finish it together!"

The finished product read:

> The sun is playing a joke on us
> First it's bright,
> Then it's night,
> Bright, bright,
> Night, night.

It was labeled, "Written by Jerry with help from the class."

One autumn day this same group was playing in the sunshine. A little girl said, "Miss A...., don't let's play for a minute. Let's just stand still and look. Everything is so pretty." So they all stood still and looked. One youngster said, "The trees have windows. You can see the sky through." "Yes," added another, "and the telephone wires, too."

"Another poem," they all cried and begged the teacher to write it down for them.

Miss A...., who was trying a creative program for the first time, marveled constantly at how many ideas her children had and how easily they came out.

This bit of verse came straight from the heart of a child in another first-grade room on a blue October day:

> Sky, sky,
> You're so blue
> I could fly
> Right up in you.

Did you ever hear a child's poem that was more genuinely from the heart than this one an eighth-grade boy wrote about his dog one day when all the children had brought their pets to school?

BERTHA

She's just a little yellow dog,
    As homely as can be.
Fat and round as any log,
    But she looks nice to me.

Her hair is scraggly and long,
    And never stays in place.
I think that she was made up wrong,
    For she has whiskers on her face.

My Grandpa says she barks too loud,
    When she goes out at night.
But who could feel the least bit proud
    Of a dog that wouldn't bark but bite?

For they say a barking dog won't bite,
    And Bertha barks a lot;
So we all think that she's all right,
    For she's the only dog we've got.

Poetry is the product of rich and unhurried living.

If you really appreciate the writing your children do, they will write more. Praise is as powerful as "Vigoro" in causing growth. "I do like that poem Susie made yesterday," will bring forth any number of new sprouts. Seeing the poem printed in the class poetry book or posted in a conspicuous place is another poem-producer. But do not make the mistake of praising and posting only the best verse. Praise and post the best lines of each child. A garden plot with a single brilliant rose bush may look loveliest to an artist. But what about all the little petunias and bachelor buttons just longing to grace a garden?

*If you want poetry to grow in your room, quietly suggest
to a child that the idea he has just expressed would make a
good poem.* Mrs. D.... has a happy, busy second grade.
During a social studies unit, a big poster was made on cotton
picking in the South. Kay, a child with great interest in
words, said one day, "I like our social studies poster. The
Negroes look like butterflies when the wind blows."

"That idea would make a nice poem, Kay," suggested
Mrs. D..... "Why don't you write one in your free time this
afternoon?" Kay did. This is what she wrote:

SOUTHERN SNOW

> I like to see the cotton,
> It looks like fluffy white snow,
> And the Negroes working in the fields
> With their bright shiny clothes
> Look like butterflies
> When the wind blows.

Notice the real poetic imagery of the lines.

*If you daily give the invitation to write, the children will
keep you well supplied with poems.* Miss H.... took her
fifth- and sixth-grade youngsters out into the first snowfall
of the year. They caught and examined the fluffy flakes. The
children talked about what snowflakes made them think of.
The poems the children made that day were especially lovely.
Perhaps it was because they went outside to meet the snow.
Five of these poems follow.

> All was still,
> But the snowflakes fell
> Like paratroops invading the land;
> Before we know it they have conquered the land,
> But then their enemy, the sun, came out
> And the snowflakes shrank sadly away.

The snow was sparkling bits of lace
Twirling, tumbling, every place.
It was a silver rainbow blue
Small shiny pearls just like the dew
As the first ones fell and hit the earth, they simply vanished,
It seemed as though the earth was famished.

They whirl and twirl,
Around they go,
And when you want to catch them,
They say, "No! No! No!"

Crumbs of heavenly bread
Falling from the sky
And when they reach the ground,
They are so little and shy.

The whirling, twirly, fluffy snowflakes
Are like velvet snow,
They make me think of floating feathers,
They come down,
And on my crown,
Then smaller and smaller they grow.

A fourth-grade teacher suggested that her pupils write
about pioneer transportation, since they had been reading
many pioneer stories. She got both stories and verse. One
child, who had previously shown no tendency to write,
handed this poem to her teacher:

PIONEER DAYS

In pioneer days
When feet were cars,
There were no trucks, trains,
Or airplanes.

In pioneer days
There were Indians crouching in woods,
And wild animals, too,
Ready to leap at you.

Notice the unusual thought in the second line.

A poetry drawer is a constant invitation to write. Hugh Mearns,[1] in his "Creative Power," tells of a drawer or box marked "Poetry" in which his children deposited their creative verse. I have known a number of teachers who have used this device, with the result that their children wrote more verse than they had written before. The shy child could hand his poem in unseen by the other children.

A little boy in the fifth grade in a rural school gave this poem quietly to his teacher one day when no one was looking.

MOONLIGHT

The silvery moon spread a glimmering glow
    On the crystal ice
And the gleaming white snow.

The stars peeping out one by one
    All were telling
The day was done.

And rabbits in flight
    Ran in the light
Of the stars and the silvery moon.

This poem shows a beautifully sensitive spirit.

Poems which find their way into the poetry drawer should be marked "Private," if the child wishes no one but the teacher to see them. Once in a while, a poem is just too personal a thing to be shown to a group. The most creative children are usually the most sensitive. They do not always want their poems shared. The poetry or story drawer will get more quantity than quality, but it gets children to write freely.

It might give the despairing teacher heart to read Longfellow's first attempt at verse:

---

[1] Mearns, Hugh, *Creative Power.* Doubleday Doran and Co., Inc., 1929, p. 24-25.

Mr. Finney had a turnip,
And it grew behind the barn,
And it grew and it grew
And the turnip did no harm.

*You will get a better quality of verse from your children
if you pay little attention to rhyme.* Poetry that your children
say unconsciously probably will not rhyme and may be nothing more or less than prose said beautifully or differently.
However, it is usually better verse than the jingle type. As you
read poetry, such as Hilda Conkling's, draw attention to the
fact that sometimes the nicest poems do not rhyme.

Notice the fresh quality of these prose poems, which were
written by children in the first, second, and fifth grades:

MY LAWN

My lawn has dandelion soldiers
That grow while I sleep.
I think they must be Nazi soldiers,
And I'm going to "get" those Nazis
With my daddy's new lawn mower.

BLUE-BIRDS

I never see any blue-birds,
About all I see is robins,
So I think there must be
A blue-bird school in the day-time.

SNOWFLAKES

Snowflakes are falling,
Snowflakes pure white,
They make a pretty blanket,
What more do you need to make a winter?

A Quiet Hour Each Week. School is such an alive place
to most youngsters that it is hard for them to sit still long
enough to write. A quiet hour each week during which each

one—even the teacher—paints, draws, models, weaves, sews, or writes is a little pool of composure in an active week. Usually soft music is played on the radio or victrola as the children work. Smiles are the only form of communication. If a child wants to help in the spelling of a word, he starts the word on the paper and leaves a space following it. The teacher is in her world too. Nobody disturbs anybody else. During the rest of the week the teacher gives ideas for the quiet hour and helps untangle snarls. It takes careful planning to have all the materials ready before the hour begins. Many good things other than creative products come out of the quiet hour.

It is a heart-warming experience to lead children in the writing of creative verse. In the poetry they write, they come nearest perhaps to letting us into the secret places of their hearts—and, for adults, that is a privilege indeed.

We must not fail them. We must not let their verses become more important to us than their thoughts. We must not become so proud of the things they write that we lose track of why they are writing. If we can help them always to be discoverers of new worlds, what more can any mortal do for another?

POETRY BOOKS THAT WILL DELIGHT YOUR CHILDREN

Aldis, Dorothy, *Before Things Happen*. New York: Putnam, 1936.

Association for Childhood Education Literature Committee, *Sung Under the Silver Umbrella*. Chicago: Macmillan, 1935. An outstanding collection for the younger children.

Barnes, Ruth A., Comp., *I Hear American Singing*. Chicago: Winston, 1937. (A collection of folk poetry)

Brewton, John E., Comp., *Gaily We Parade*. Chicago: Macmillan, 1940. (Poems about people)

Brewton, John E., Comp., *Under the Tent of the Sky*. Chicago: Macmillan, 1937. (Poems about animals)

Chute, Marchette G., *Rhymes About the Country*. Chicago: Macmillan, 1941 (Charming verse for little children)

De la Mare, Walter, *A Child's Day*. New York: Henry Holt, also Cadmus, 1923. (Primary)

De la Mare, Walter, *Peacock Pie*. New York: Henry Holt, 1936. (Primary children)

Gillis, A., and Benet, William, Comps. *Poems for Modern Youth*. Boston: Houghton Mifflin, 1938. (A collection for junior high school)

Hufford, Grace T., and Others, Comps., *My Poetry Book*. Philadelphia: John C. Winston, 1934. (An unusual and large collection of modern poems of all types loved by children)

Milne, A. A., *Now We Are Six*. (New York: E. P. Dutton, 1927. (Primary children)

Milne, A. A., *When We Were Very Young*. New York: E. P. Dutton, 1924. (Delightful English poetry)

Sandburg, Carl, *Early Moon*. New York: Harcourt Brace, 1930. (Inimitable poems on the child's level)

Sechrist, Elizabeth Hough, Comp., *One Thousand Poems for Children*. Philadelphia: McCrae Smith, 1946.

Thompson, Blanche J., ed., *Silver Pennies*. Chicago: Macmillan, 1925. (A collection of fanciful poems for intermediate and upper grades)

Thompson, Blanche J., ed., *More Silver Pennies*. Chicago: Macmillan, 1938.

Thorn, Alice G., Comp., *Singing Words*. New York: Scribner's, 1941.

Tippett, James S., *I Know Some Little Animals*. New York: Harper, 1941. (Clever poems)

Untermeyer, Louis, ed., *Stars to Steer by*. New York: Harcourt, Brace and Co., 1941.

Untermeyer, Louis, ed., *This Singing World for Younger Children*. New York: Harcourt, Brace and Co., 1926. (An unusual collection for all children)

CHILDREN'S OWN POETRY

Conkling, Hilda, *Poems by a Little Girl*. New York: Frederick A. Stokes, 1920.

Conkling, Hilda, *Shoes of the Wind*. New York: Frederick A. Stokes, 1922.

Robert, Bertha, and Beckman, Aneta, Comp., *Children's Voices*. New York: Silver Burdette, 1939.

Chapter III

Rhymes and Reasons

Children need no boats or planes

In order to fly;

Their minds have sails,

Their thoughts have wings

That seek the open sky.

Chapter III
Rhymes and Reasons

ONCE UPON A TIME there was a forgetful gardener who plowed and cultivated a plot of ground with loving care. But he forgot to plant any seeds. The sun shone kindly on the fresh earth and the rain watered it gently.

When the forgetful gardener discovered that he had planted no seeds, it was too late to make amends. But, strange to say, as spring advanced his garden was not bare. There had been seeds asleep in the earth since last fall where the parent plants had scattered them. These seeds had fought their way through the dark earth, but, save for the weeds, they were the only plants in the man's garden.

When harvest time came, the crop was small indeed. The gardener wondered if the time he had spent in tending the few plants had really been worth his while.

Teachers are gardeners. When they try to grow poetry plants, they often feel with the forgetful gardener that they work too hard for a small crop. The climate of their rooms may be just right for growing; the children may be responsive; they themselves may be conscientious and hard-working; and they may try all the methods listed in the preceding chapter to produce more and better poetry. But still the crop may be too small.

Reading poetry to the children, appreciating things together, giving the daily invitation to write, having a quiet hour each week, and providing a poetry drawer will grow more and better poetry. However, unless the teacher is an extraordinary one, _not all the children will write poetry_.

Do we want all the children to write? Are all the children able to write? Let us think the matter over together.

29

First let us consider our purposes in helping children to write. Writing develops the personality, gives children something to be proud of, and provides an emotional release.

As we consider our purposes, it seems that the writing of poetry is fruitful enough in results to warrant our trying to get all the children to want to write it. Chapter II listed the gentle, more subtle ways of getting children to write. If a teacher has an above-average group of children, she may never have to use more obvious means of stimulation. But, after a time, many teachers discover that some of the best things children write in school come as the result of assignments. Many creative people are not self-starting. The need for food and shelter has been the none too gentle push that compelled many of our greatest adult writers to produce. Assignments are the teacher's particular type of push to writers who are not adult.

A modern teacher considers the individual child in making her assignments in poetry writing. She never assigns a poem to be written by all the children. She gives each member of the class a choice between writing a poem and writing a story. She never narrows the subject in such a way that some children will find nothing in their thoughts or experiences to write about. In other words, the wise teacher will provide for individual differences, but she will sometimes make assignments common to all. From these assignments will come some of the best poems she has ever received from children. Human nature needs pushes if it would reach beyond itself. But poetry pushes are gentle, and they are more a leading than a pushing.

Assignments in verse-writing are preceded by an actual preparing of the ground. A whole class does not write without preparation. Verse-making may develop out of a unit of school work or out of an experience the whole class has had. It may be an outgrowth of a season of the year. The assignment may come about in numerous ways, but it will be more fruitful if the teacher prepares the class for writing.

She may read to them a variety of poems as a background to the subject on which they are writing. This is not done in order that they will have something to copy or imitate, but in order that the grandeur and simplicity of thoughts well said may in time exert an influence on their sense of taste in poetry. It is interesting to notice the difference in the quality of poetry preferred by a class that has been used to an ascending scale of poetry reading from kindergarten on. Taste develops slowly, but surely, through a continuous living with the best.

The teacher preparing a class for writing will discuss the subject with them. Through that thought-sharing there will come a deepening and a widening of the stream of ideas and the opening of new channels of thought. Those who came to class with no ideas will go away with ideas. Strange new words and new shades of meaning of familiar words will come out of this thinking together. It is not ideas that children lack; it is the discriminating vocabulary to express them. One cannot travel to the stars in a wheelbarrow, or speak of his journey there in the words of the field. (Chapter VII can help teachers to strengthen their vocabularies.) One might call this preparation period a seeing-together. For some it strengthens the vision; for others it provides glasses to correct the vision; it helps others to see afar.

After the preparation, will all the pupils complete the assignment and write poems? The answer in most classes is a definite "no." A few have no ability; a small number have no powers of expression; and one or two have no interest in this particular subject. The teacher will have provided for the few with no ability by assigning either a poem or a story or by permitting the use of some medium other than writing. The small number with no powers of expression will struggle hard to write something to please the teacher if they like her; if they don't like her, they will smile limply or shrug off the assignment. The teacher can provide for the third group by offering either a choice of subjects or several phases of the same subject.

A sixth-grade teacher, with whom I have worked closely over a period of years, gets every child in her large classes to write. She is not a particularly creative teacher, but she is a very appreciative, understanding person. Because of her consistently good results with class poetry assignments, I am giving you the privilege that I had of sitting in one of her classes on a bright spring morning.

Said Miss W. . . . to her class:

"Since we went on that hike last week to meet spring, I have been so full of the feeling of spring that I can hardly teach school. When I ought to have had my mind solidly on arithmetic, I have found my thoughts going right out of the window and down to the lake. I can tell that you are feeling the same way. I've tried to give you (and to give myself) opportunities to express our feelings about spring. We've hiked and painted and made up a song together. I have read you spring poetry each morning. We've expressed spring in many ways. Let's write about it tomorrow. Your writing may take any form you wish: a poem, a story, or words to a song. Your thoughts may take the form of a description of something you have heard or seen or imagined or felt. It may be you talking, a bird or a flower talking, or a story talking. The form is unimportant—*but tell how you feel about spring*. I know you are feeling something. I'd rather have two lines that tell how you really feel than twelve lines on what some one else feels.

"I'll write something, too, for tomorrow. I think mine will take the form of a poem. I already know how I'm going to begin it. It won't be very good, but it will be mine."

I wish I had written down Miss W's exact words, but I was too busy listening to do any writing. I have, however, conveyed the spirit of her assignment to you. As you may have guessed, every child of the twenty-five came forth with an offering, and twenty wrote poems.

Almost any teacher could write a poem as simple as Miss W's proved to be the next day.

> "I don't want to teach today,
> I want to run away—far away;
> I'd like to put away my glasses
> And everything that pertains to classes,
> I want to have fun in the sun.
> I want to spend hours
> Getting the backache picking spring flowers.
> Turn around, feet,
> Come on back,
> I have a job to do!"

Of course the children loved it—they love Miss W. If you can't be humble and share your thoughts honestly with your children, how can you expect them to share theirs with you?

IDEAS THAT MAY HELP YOU IN
MAKING
DEFINITE ASSIGNMENTS

Poems which result from a unit of work. When children are preparing a program as a culminating activity of a unit of work in the social studies or science, poems pop out as naturally as violets through the grass.

Notice the beauty of this chant composed by a fourth-grade class as a part of its study of the Navaho Indians.

CHANT FOR RAIN

Great Spirit, send us rain.
  Our people are starving and in need of grain.
We have not had rain for many a moon.
  Great Spirit, send us rain.
We've offered our corn and we've offered our grain.
  Great Spirit, send us rain.
We are weaving blankets for you, too.
  Great Spirit, send us rain.
Silver bracelets with turquoise blue
  These, great Spirit, we offer you.
Three fine sheep and a new born lamb,
  The best we have in all the land.
Great Spirit, send us rain.
  Great Spirit, send us rain.

In the same program a little girl crouched under a loom which held a Navaho rug and told its life story. So moving were her words that one could feel the pathos of the life of a Navaho woman. The program centered around a play which the children had also written.

A second-grade class had fun making this "Chant of the Cotton Workers" as they were studying and dramatizing the story of clothing.

CHANT OF THE COTTON WORKERS

April! April!
We plant cotton in April.
We plant the cotton seeds.

Rain, rain! Come down, rain!
Come down to make the seeds grow.
Make the cotton seeds grow.

Sun, sun! Great sun!
Shine and make the seeds grow.
Make the cotton seeds grow.

Hoe, hoe! Weed and hoe,
While King Cotton grows.

Bright sun, hot sun.
More showers, cotton flowers,
As King Cotton grows.

Spray, spray, spray!
Come, planes, spray!
Spray the summer snow,
So the weevils will not grow.

Green bells. Brown.
Pop! Fluff! Fluff!
Fluffy cotton, summer snow.
Time to pick the cotton now.
Pick! Pick! Pick!

Notice how repetition and the "sing-song" of Negro melodies affect the rhythm of the chant. Notice, too, how the article from *My Weekly Reader* telling about spraying cotton from airplanes has interested the children.

This same group churned cream into butter in a glass jar and composed a chant as they worked—talking to the butter and begging it to form.

Units on transportation are productive of verse. Children are more likely to write these individually than as a group.

The following two poems show how small boys (grades 6 and 4) can get really eloquent about airplanes.

AIRPLANES

The plane was invented by the Wrights;
It had very many successful flights.
It was a pretty sight to see
That plane go by so fast and free.

ON THE LAKE

I saw an airplane flying
High and free;
I'll bet to it we looked like
A bunch of baby possums on the sea;
Our boat was the mother possum
And we were her babies three.

Notice in the second bit of verse how a science lesson of the month before was brought into the picture.

The prize poem from a transportation unit is this delightful bit of four lines by a girl named Marjorie:

> The boat says he likes to go swimming,
> He says it washes his back;
> But my! when he turns over,
> He gets a nice whack!

Can't you just imagine that Marjorie, a fourth-grade pupil, is watching a little boat which is moored to a pier along the lake and is getting its back slapped!

Poems which result from tours of the senses. Did you ever take a smelling tour? One spring or fall morning when the air is yeasty with many smells, go for a hike with your children. Pay particular attention to the smells in the air and try to identify them. Come back to the class room and change the smells into words. The children will be startled to find how lean their vocabularies are of smell-identifying words.

The identification may go slowly at first, the progress depending on the backgrounds of the children. When feasible, use dictionaries. Find new smell-identifying words together. The teacher's contribution to the class comes in designating shades of word-meaning and in reading a few sentences from the classics which describe smells. This one is typical:[1] "A smell like an eatinghouse and a pastry cook's next door to each other with a laundry next door to that! That was the pudding!" A teacher will, of course, add to the list of words suggested by the children. There is a tendency among a number of teachers to gather words from the class without enriching the list with their own contributions. In such a procedure the level of the class does not rise.

---

[1] Dickens, Charles, *A Christmas Carol*. The Atlantic Monthly Press, 1920, p. 94.

The discussion and the dictionary work may bring out such phrases as the following:

> The acrid smell of green wood or leaves burning.
> The wet, moldy smell of decaying leaves.
> The fresh smell of clean winds.
> The aromatic smell of pine needles.
> The pungent smell of smoke.

In a class notebook add to these smell-identifying words as the days go by. Literature will be a rich source of new words.

Two possible creative writing assignments may come from a smelling-tour.

1. Let the class make together a poem beginning and ending with such a line as "I Like Smells," and let each child contribute a line about the smell he likes best. Two typical lines are:

> "I like the smell of my sister's perfume—it's just like flowers."
> "I like the smell of the basement on wash day—it's so clean."

If a child has no contribution, just go on to the next. You cannot force creative speech.

2. Ask each child to write a poem or a paragraph about a smell or smells he likes. Be sure that this assignment comes after vocabulary study in class.

Notice the genuineness in these two samples from a seventh-grade class in a junior high school. One is:

> I think of leaves red and yellow turning
> And smell the brown ones that are burning.
> I think of corn stalks drying in the fields—
> Stalks that corn no longer yields.
> I think of pumpkins gold and yellow,
> Pumpkins all so ripe and mellow.
> I think of gardens being spaded,
> And report cards being graded!

The second sample is:

> I walk home from school in the crisp autumn air—
> Take off my coat and hang it up.
> I smell the warm dinner waiting for me.
> Then all through the meal I wonder—
> Why does everything seem different to me?
> It all is very queer and puzzling,
> Then suddenly I realize that October is here.

If your class is too large to be taken on a hike, use open windows and the imagination in lieu of the hike—and the same results may come.

A sound tour is conducted on the same principle as a smelling tour. A fourth-grade group listened to the big clock in their own school room and made individual contributions on things of which the ticking reminded them. The teacher, who was doing her first year of teaching, was amazed at the number and variety of picturesque contributions. Notice that, with the change of a tense or a word here and there, these individual lines might be fashioned into a real poem.

Things of which a clock reminds me:

> A boat rocking back and forth in the wind.
> Fairies softly marching.
> Its ticking tells a story.
> Chattering of my teeth.
> Wooden shoes on a cobblestone walk.
> Tapping of a woodpecker on a telephone post.
> Snipping of the barber's shears.
> Horse munching hay.
> Flapping of a circus tent entrance flap against the tent.
> Soft tapping of drums.
> Like snowflakes falling softly to the ground one by one.
> Mysterious sound of the wind whistling through the leaves.
> Ghosts walking very quietly.
> Flowers swaying back and forth in the summer breeze.
> Clop, clop of a horse's shoes on the pavement.

Rain softly falling on a tin roof.
Tap, tap of a shoemaker's hammer.
Sailboat rocking back and forth in the wind.
Even swinging of a woodchopper's axe.

After class several children tried individual poems. Marlene contributed these four lines:

THE CLOCK

The little kitchen clock
Says "Tick, tick, tock."
It sounds like a little girl
Walking in a sock.

A <u>sight tour</u> may be taken via a window, and may be followed by group vocabulary work.

A sixth-grade class made this poem together after a window tour. It contains three observations unusual to children of eleven:

THOUGHTS OF SPRING

When we look out of the window at school,
We see tulips,
Brave little fellows, in crimson and yellows.
Young tender, yellow-green leaves,
Waving in the spring's fresh breeze.
Great white clouds against the blue,
Purple violets hidden in among the dew.
Lacy shadows crawling slow,
Catching birds that come and go.
Little dandelions, rich and mellow,
Most of them a bright spring yellow.
Shadowed tree trunks hide the ground
With their foliage swinging round.
As we sit here watching Time
And making up this fancy rhyme,
How we wish that school would end,
So our fun would all begin.

A third grade at another school got this cooperative result:

FROM THE SCHOOL WINDOW

When I look out the window each day,
I look up at the grayish sky,
I see a squirrel leap from tree to tree;
As I look at trees they look like people
But they're only branches that hang in the way.
They bow to Mr. Wind as he goes by,
And then they dance and sigh, sigh, sigh!

Another effective way of conducting a sight tour is to ask each member of the class to spend at least fifteen minutes by himself during the week under a bush or tree quietly watching. If the "spade-work" before the class really awakens interest, you may get surprising results.

This is Joanne's contribution:

WHEN I WAS ON A HILLSIDE

Sitting on a hillside on a summer's day,
Thinking of things to do,
Sitting on a hillside in the month of May,
Looking at the sky above so blue.

Listening to the birds as they sing,
Singing of this lovely day in Spring.

A poem of best lines. This poem is really a mosaic of many children's work. It comes as an outgrowth of a center of interest. Perhaps your children have been studying airplanes. A few days before, they have written either stories or poems trying to express how an airplane flies. A committee and yourself (or just you, if creative writing is in its early stages in your room) pick out the most creative line from each child's poem. These lines are either written on the board or given to each child on a mimeographed sheet. The class, then, either creates a new poem from these suggestions or puts the lines together with slight alterations to form a new poem. The class does not know, of course, by whom the original lines were written.

This poem was written in this way:

> Down the hillside came my sheep
> All black and white in endless line;
> I love to care for my fleecy sheep
> For I'm the hillside shepherd boy.
>
> In the meadow's deep green grass
> I see the flowery stars,
> I play my harp and sing my songs
> For God is watching over me.

The idea sheet. For years I avoided using any definite suggestions in making poetry assignments. I noticed, of course, that many children had no ideas at all.

"True creativeness comes from within," I argued with myself. "It would be wrong to give any teacher-suggestions."

But the fact that some children continued to get ideas from each other and from books was often brought to my attention. Suddenly one day I realized that I had not been thinking very straight. I studied my group of friends and acquaintances. Where did they get their ideas for their hats, their dresses, or their knitting or crotcheting? I found that only a few used original patterns. The majority got their ideas hither and yon; from books, magazines, store windows, and friends. Also, I noticed that, through adding a bow here or removing a feather there, they wove a bit of themselves into their copy work. When finished, the products looked quite different from the original ones, even though the ideas had come from outside themselves.

I sat down and did some thinking. How could I furnish ideas to the uncreative without fostering pattern work and stifling originality? The idea sheet was the result. Instead of stifling creativity, the suggestions on the sheet released it for the children who write well but lack ideas. The few real writers in the class used the sheet either sparingly or not at all, and *every child in the class made at least a four-line contribution*.

The following sheet was used during a unit of work on air travel:

> If you have no ideas for a poem these may help you:
>
> a. You are making a test flight before you receive your wings. How do you feel? How does your plane look and feel? What thoughts are you think-ing?
>
> b. An airplane is like a bird. What does it remind you of? In what way?
>
> c. There are many children in the airplane family. What are their names, and how are they different? Where do they live?
>
> d. You are up in the clouds on a mission over a foreign land. It is a beauiful morning. All at once you see enemy planes coming toward you. What do you do? How do you feel? What happens?
>
> e. I wonder how things look to an airplane far up in the sky?

If you prepare an idea sheet, urge your pupils to use ideas of their own. They will usually prove to be better ideas than yours.

In Chapter VII you will find all the material that came in as a result of using the foregoing sheet with twelve ordinary sixth graders who had never used one before. They used the ideas as a springboard only. Each child's contribution is given in the exact words of the child with spelling and punc-tuation changes. These changes seemed necessary because the children who wrote the verse might be embarrassed later to see mistakes which they have now outgrown.

It is better to read the ideas to the children than to give them the mimeographed sheet. This may be because the sheet is indicative of an assignment and there is a tendency to

follow the suggestions rather than to use the ideas as spring-
boards.

Exercises in rhyme. Some suggestions for developing
rhyme follow:

a. In kindergarten and in the first four grades, it is
   fun to start verses for children and let them finish
   them *orally*. The oral rhymes are of very little
   value as verse, but the exercises give the children
   facility in handling rhyme and sensing rhythm.

b. Bouncing a ball to rhyming words is popular with
   little youngsters. They may start with the word
   sled and may bounce the ball for every rhyming
   work they can think of. Sometimes they think of
   Ned, red, bed, led, dead, and Fred before they
   run out of rhyming words.

c. The use of number rhymes is a version of "one-
   two, buckle my shoe." Such rhymes may be sung
   or said. The numbers from one through ten are
   given to ten children, each of whom makes a rhyme
   about his number. You will get such rhymes as
   "One, one! What have I done?" "Two, two! What
   can you do?" "Three, three! Birds in a tree." "Four,
   four! I want some more!" This game is also adapted
   to ball bouncing and may be continued as long
   as the child can think of rhyming words.

d. Children in primary grades like to make rhymes
   about color. The class chants, "Red, red, what is
   red?" or names some other color. Any volunteer
   answers with a rhyming phrase. This goes slowly at
   first; but, after the children get acquainted with
   the idea of the game, the words come almost at
   once. Sample rhymes are:
   "Red, red! What is red?" My bed.
   "Blue, blue! What is blue?" A shoe.

e. Primary children have lots of fun with question
   and answer rhymes, such as the following:
   "No wonder John is wise; he asks so may why's."

Let the group think of some why's John may have asked:

"Why can't we have pie every meal?"
"Why does velvet have a plushy feel?"
"Why can't I have a little brother?"
"Why can't my teacher be my mother?"
"Why do woodpeckers knock on wood?"
"Why does ice-cream taste so good?"

This is not only a "limbering-up" exercise, but will tell an observing teacher what her children are thinking about.

Another similar game is to ask a question and let the children give rhyming answers. Examples are:

Teacher: "Why is a rabbit's nose so twitchy?"
Pupil: "Do you suppose that it is itchy?"
Teacher: "Why are violets always blue?"
Pupil: "They look at the sky and get that way too."
Teacher: "Why do leaves come out in spring?"
Pupil: "They want to hear the blue birds sing."

Some day, when you are in a good mood, let the children ask the question and you give the rhyming answer. Be prepared for such teasers as, "Why are teachers always cross?" You'll just have to be a good sport and come back with, "It's lots of work to be the boss!"

If you yourself can't rhyme, let the children furnish both the questions and the answers.

    f.   For sheer fun and for practice in rhyme "without reason," I know of no better exercise than making limericks. The rhyme-scheme for this type of jingle is 1, 1, 2, 2, 1 (the last line rhymes with the first two and the two middle lines, slightly shorter, rhyme with each other). Many children like to make limericks about themselves. These two from a sixth-grade girl are typical elementary-school limericks:

JIM

There was an old man named Jim
Who was full of vigor and vim;
He could read the paper,
He could cut many a caper,
And no one could get the best of him.

JOE

There was a young man named Joe,
At work he was very slow;
He poked and he puttered,
He stammered and stuttered,
And so he didn't make any dough.

Probably the best outcome of this type of exercise is getting a feeling for line balance. Consider the line, "Why can't we have pie every meal?" If this line is written with *each* instead of *every*, the line would then be thrown off balance. Write such a line on the board and let the class "sing-song" it to get the feel of balance. The children will often ask for this game.

Surprise and wishes. Children love surprises. They love surprise poems, too. Read them poems with surprise endings. As a child tells of a surprise he had, the teacher can suggest his writing about it. These surprises might be the basis for surprise poems:

a. You look under a setting hen and find—not eggs but four black kittens.

b. You are having an exciting adventure. Finally you wake up with a start and find it is only a dream.

c. A corporal in the army orders fifty soldiers inside an old house to surrender. He leads the men to think that they are surrounded. When they come out with their hands up, they find that one man has captured them.

d. John is taking the presents out of his Christmas stocking one by one. In the toe of the sock, shivering with fear, is ....

Many children have a secret silly wish; most adults have too. A teacher of a fourth-grade class used this original verse about her silly wish, to get her children to write about theirs:

When I'm grown up
And am rich as can be,
And can have everything that I wish or see,
Out in the front yard
Where there's lots of shade
I want to have a fountain
That squirts pink lemonade.

Favorite "gripes." The *Plaint of the Camel*,[1] a humorous poem by Charles Edward Carryl, expresses a camel's disgust with his shape and his food and the world in general. After reading the poem to the children, discuss with them their favorite plaints. Ask them to write about their gripes in poems, stories, or songs. (Note: The teacher would have fun trying this one herself.)

Poems that express wonder and fear. If there is true rapport between you and your pupils, and if your children are used to writing verse, ask them to spend one "quiet hour" writing about their greatest fear or wonder or mystery.

Talk with the group about some of the problems that are common to most children. Also remember to announce that these poems will be for your eyes alone if the children so indicate on their papers.

The problems and fears in some of these poems are apparent. In others, one can only guess what feelings lie behind the words. The four that follow were written by pupils in grades 4, 5, 6, and 8.

---

[1] Brewton, John E., *Under the Tent of the Sky.* The Macmillan Company, 1947, p. 18-19.

FRIGHTENING RAIN

The clouds were like fighting animals,
And the rain was pattering on the window pane.
The splashing of the pupils' feet and the
Slashing of the lightning outside,
Makes it so frightening outside at night time.

NO PLAY

I take care of Bob all day,
And never seem to have time to play.
But when the war is won,
I'll then have time to play and run.
All the mothers will be glad
And no one ever again will be sad.

BIRDS

Birds are shy,
They aren't like boys or girls,
I saw a bird,
He never went
Where he was not told.

HOME?

War is a terrible thing
With all the wounded and dead,
And disease spreading as if it had wings—
People wandering around, unfed.
Many are trapped under buildings
Either to starve or to smother,
Children, unnoticed, start weeping and crying,
Looking for father and mother.
The dead are lying everywhere,
Never more to rise,
But even if their proud country falls,
Their spirit never dies.

Kathryn, in Grade 3 and eight years old, has written her wonderings into one of the finest children's poems in this collection.

I WONDER

I wonder if when children pray,
If their prayers travel all day,
Or if one stops to say,
"Hello, Mr. Cloud, may I come in today?"
I wonder if other children wonder
If their prayers go hither and yonder.

Poems for special days. This type of poem is found so
often in schools that it is not necessary to devote much space
to explaining it. It is well to put the poems of holiday time
on a purely voluntary basis in order that no youngster will
lose his zest for holidays because of the writing that goes with
them. I heard a boy groan in the hall one day, "Mother's
Day—another poem!" That sentence speaks for itself. Moti-
vated holiday verse, such as a few lines for a valentine each
child has made or a poem for a Mother's Day gift, provides a
different sort of incentive to write. But even these should
be purely voluntary offerings. This Thanksgiving Prayer was
a class cooperative poem to be used at a Thanksgiving program. Each pupil and the teacher suggested one line, which
was a voluntary contribution.

A THANKSGIVING PRAYER

Lord, we thank Thee—
For saving this nation from destruction,
For freedom and peace in this land of ours,
For brave men and women who have gone to serve our country
To keep that freedom everlasting.

For the beautiful things around us,
For plentiful crops and soil to make them grow,
For valuable materials stored within the earth
Which keep the wheels of industry turning.

For homes and loving parents,
For brothers, sisters, and kind friends,

For doctors, nurses and dentists
Who give their lives to keep us well and happy.

For giving us a chance to earn our living,
For pleasures when our work is done,
For men with minds so great and brilliant
Who have made this world a better place in which to live.

For a sound mind and healthy body,
For life and strength to carry on,
For everything we've ever had or will have,
Lord, we thank Thee! Amen.

The following two poems are from grade 1:

HALLOWE'EN

Smoke men come on Hallowe'en,
Black cats and goblins, too.
Witches with big green eyes
Look you through and through.

MOTHER

I love you, dear mother,
There is no other,
Your eyes are so kind,
Your voice is so sweet.

From grades 4 and 6 come these:

HALLOWE'EN

Ghosts and goblins flying overhead,
I think I would rather be in bed.

EASTER

The Easter bunny pink and white
He comes while I'm asleep at night;
He fills my basket heaped up high
With eggs made pretty in dye;
There are candy ones, too,
And flowers gay for you.

Poems suggested by pictures. After a picture has been discussed, give the invitation for poem writing to those who are interested. Only a few will respond, but those few may write very worth-while verse.

> Whoo! Whoo! the wind is coming up.
> We'll be caught in the wind.
> We'll twirl and whirl
> Whoo! the wind is coming up!

The fourth-grade child who wrote this was impressed by the picture of a sail boat in a storm. He is used to watching the boats on the lake near his home.

The following poem by a boy in fourth grade who loves the water was written about a picture studied in art class. Note how children are interested in pictures which remind them of personal experiences. We must study a variety of pictures in order to reach all of the children.

> Boats bobbing up and down,
> The tide was coming in.
> Grey gulls are flying
> Over fishing schooners,
> Hoping for fish
> The fishermen might have thrown in.

The following poem was written by an eighth-grade boy after seeing a dog picture displayed on the bulletin board during "Be Kind to Animals" week.

ALONE

> One lone cocker spaniel
> On our doorstep sat.
> His ribs were showing plainly
> That he wasn't very fat.
>
> He, evidently, had broken his leg—
> Or else he'd sprained a limb,
> But nobody worried or cared at all,
> And the snow beat down on him.

He didn't knock or scratch the door,
He didn't even bark,
All he did was hope and wait,
All by himself in the dark.

For all I know that poor little dog
May still be roaming the street.
All I wish is that I had taken him in
And had given him a place to sleep.

Magazine pictures help many children to express their personal experiences in an impersonal way.

Ballads. Children have so much fun listening to and acting out ballads. Beginning with the fifth grade, these poems are universal favorites. Encourage children to write ballads about war heroes or pirates whom they admire. Some of them would enjoy changing an old folk tale into a ballad. This is easy to do for the following reasons:

1. A ballad tells a story.
2. It usually has a swinging rhyme.
3. It often has made-up jingling words at intervals throughout the poem.

Ballads were songs at one time when the wandering minstrels sang them from castle to castle. A ballad program to which the mothers are invited is a novel idea. Ballads are read and dramatized, and their histories are read. The whole program may hinge about an old castle which is being visited by minstrels. A chorus sings old ballads, and the children read their own original ballads. It is fun to get the mothers interested before the program and ask any who wish to bring old favorites to read or sing. A few mothers in some communities may wish to read original ballads of their own.

Talking poems. Many children write better if they have an imaginary something to talk to. Eunice is talking to the Koala bear she modeled in clay and painted when her sixth-grade class was studying Australia. The bear seems real to Eunice. She got the most comical expression on its clay face.

MY KOALA BEAR

You are a comical bear
With velvety silk-like hair.
You like to sit in a tree
And make funny faces at me.
Your ears are floppy, your eyes bright,
Your feet are clawy, your face a sight
You look like a teddy bear
That someone won at a fair.
You are carefree, happy, and gay,
Waiting for someone to come and play.

Note that adding an *are* before bright in the fifth line would make the line smooth.

By this time you are undoubtedly convinced that there is much any teacher can do, not only to get children to love poetry but to write it as well. Children's verse does not always grow wild like rubber trees in the Amazon swamps. It as often comes from an orderly assignment made by an understanding teacher much in the way in which our best rubber is cultivated in the plantations of the East Indies.

You are the key person in poetry production. You provide the climate of the school room. You are the sun, the rain, and the gardener. Poetry doesn't just happen to most children, unless you do something about it. But even you cannot produce one poem if there is none in the heart of the child. What a mystery, growth and life are. And you and I are privileged to have a part in it.

Chapter IV

Tall Tales and
Short Tellers

All day they sail with the marines

Or with guerillas roam;

At night, scarred and gory,

Streaked with dirt and with glory,

They come bringing their tales back home.

Chapter IV

Tall Tales and
Short Tellers

THE FOLLOWING is exactly as told by five-year-old Jerry to a senior kindergarten class:

"The fire bell rang and the man was eating the leg of a chicken. He grabbed it and ran into the fire station and 'Zing!' he went down the road.

When the fire was over he came back and went back to the fire station and it rang again. Two times it rang. Next time a different bell rang. He jumped into the engine again. He ran down the road.

He went back and slept.

The chief had a dog and a cat and baby ones.

The bell rang again. Next time the bell rang AGAIN! He had to go four times.

They slipped on their boots. They zipped down the road. The engine went right through the stop-and-go signs.

A different bell rang and another fire came in a big fat building. And a man was sleeping in bed. He didn't know it. The firemen took him out. They saved him. The ambulance came after him.

Next one they found a dog—a bulldog on the road. The fire engine ran over it. It was dead. The firemen buried him in some sand."

Jerry's eyes shone. He was in his element. There was nothing he liked better than telling stories. This kindergarten teacher was nice. She liked to hear stories. His mother never had time to listen, or else she said, "Oh, Jerry, don't tell such whoppers." But this teacher was different. She told you to watch for stories on the way home from school. She said that squirrels and birds and dogs were acting out stories all along the street.

And yesterday she had taken the whole kindergarten to the fire-house. The fireman took the engine out just on purpose when there really wasn't a fire. He, Jerry, had got to slide down the fireman's pole. He had been a little scared, but it was fun.

He had wanted to talk and talk about that fire station. He wanted to stop everybody he met yesterday and say, "I just slid down the fireman's pole." But no one wanted to listen. Everybody was busy. But Miss Brown—she was different. She had this picture up on the story board the first thing today. It was a fast picture. The fireman was on his way to a fire. He must have been at the supper table when the fire came because he was eating a chicken leg.

And now he, Jerry, was telling a story all about the fireman to the class. The teacher seemed to know that he was all swelled up inside with a story because she looked at him the first thing and said, "Jerry has a story to tell us about this fireman."

And now Jerry was all done with the story, and he felt empty and good inside. Jim had offered him his red top to play with at play time, and John, the biggest boy, had walked home a little way with him after school.

And, best of all, Miss Brown was putting his story in the kindergarten book. It would be in tomorrow beside the picture—his own story about the fireman eating the chicken leg.

Jerry tried skipping all the way home. His legs did better tonight. He guessed it was because he had told such a good story. He guessed that good story-tellers could skip. He guessed they could be firemen, too, when they grew up.

Perhaps the greatest thing a teacher can do to help her children write stories is to teach them to see. Someone has said that a writer is a "see-er." He sees more and clearer and farther below the surface than other people see. Charles

Dickens was such a writer. He saw the little things in the people he met that pointed out what kind of people they really were. A look in the eye, a gesture of the hand, or a reflex action in the cheek told Charles Dickens the story behind the man. That was why this famous author always had a story—he knew that wherever people were there was a story. He was a "see-er."

Beginning in kindergarten, a good teacher can help to enlarge the vision of her pupils—the vision of both their eyes and their hearts. She can do this best by looking at them with the eyes of the heart. She can notice when they are "edgy" and short-tempered or "full of fidgets," and can handle them carefully on those days. She will know the days when great happiness floods the pages of the texts with too bright a light for studying. She will look behind the action for the reason for the action.

The children will notice how she treats others, too. Perhaps the principal has just been in and has spoken sharply to the group. "I believe Miss M. is tired today," the teacher observes when the principal has gone. "She probably had something hard to settle this morning. You children talk it over among yourselves and see what you can do to help her today. Do you suppose, Bobby, that we might give her half of the flowers you brought me this morning? Flowers have a way of lighting up a whole day." Many teachers are greatly beloved for no other quality than their power to see.

Children can come to know each other through the understanding of book characters and why they did as they did.

"What do you think Huckleberry Finn would have done in this situation?" I heard an intermediate teacher ask her class one day. "Why do you think so?" was her next question. Such an imaginative exercise develops judgment of character—and no quality is more needed in this age when factions are trying so hard to understand each other.

Studying pictured faces and trying to judge pictured situations are other ways of sharpening children's perceptions. Hoffman's picture of "Christ Among the Doctors" is an excellent study of facial expressions. Get your fifth- and sixthgrade pupils to try to imagine what each man is saying and what the young Jesus is answering.

Magazine-cover faces reveal many characteristics. Before the children write the story the picture tells, let them discuss the probable characteristics of the people. Let them guess what has gone before and what might come after. Be sure not to let them come to any definite conclusions, however.

As the teacher walks along the street with a pupil or two, such remarks as "That old house looks ready to cry" or "What a kind face that old gentleman has!" will do much to open children's eyes and get them to see things with a writer's vision.

A teacher who uses comparisons in her daily conversation will soon have pupils whose speech is more picturesque. Comparisons depend wholly upon the quality of seeing. Examples are: "The clouds seem to be playing tag today; I just saw one catch another one," and "Those dandelions look like freckles on the lawn." Such comparisons will bring out the remarks which children have already been thinking, but which they have felt reticent about saying. Write the best samples of picturesque speech where the class can see them and think about them. Encourage the children to use picturesque speech.

The greatest thing a child can say of a teacher is, "She taught me to see." Even if not one of your pupils turns out to be a writer of stories, all will have lived more fully from having had greater vision.

You will have no trouble getting your children to write stories. You may have more trouble getting them stopped to do their arithmetic than you will have getting them started to write. The same warm, leisurely climate that will produce poetry will even more readily produce stories, since stories are hardier plants and grow more easily than poems.

Children will write many stories; but, unless the teacher plans carefully, they will have little variety in their story-writing. The rest of this chapter deals with various ways teachers have found profitable in developing the many phases of story-telling. You probably will have several to add to the list. The next chapter will help you to improve children's story-writing.

A writer's corner. Is there a quiet corner of your school room or an adjoining alcove where, behind a colorful screen, a child may be alone as he writes a story?

The cardboard screen may be decorated to suggest a castle tower and be labeled "Tower Room." There is something intriguing about that title. It suggests the traveling cloak of the little lame prince and the magic carpet of the Arabian Nights. It suggests the importance, too, of being a writer. It will encourage the writing of stories in your room.

Perhaps one panel of your screen is a bulletin board painted in a soft, neutral color. Only one type of thing at a time appears on this panel each week—an invitation to write. At Hallowe'en time a jolly picture, mounted in contrasting color, calls to the children with the caption, "What Story Do I Suggest to You?" Sometimes a variety of autumn pictures are labeled, "Which of These Is Your Story?" or, "Tell About Your Hallowe'en Experience." Perhaps the panel holds the single picture of a wrinkled grandmother with the words, "Once Upon a Time." Some weeks there is no picture at all, but a series of intriguing titles is listed on the panel under the heading, "Which Is the Title of Your Story?"

When the children are studying pioneer life, an old shawl may be draped on a small table against the panel. "I Have a Story to Tell" may be the words above it. Instead of the shawl, a spinning wheel or an antique vase may be used.

There is a convenient story box near-by, with a generous mouth to take the stories which the children drop in. Each Monday the eyes of the children go naturally to the "writer's panel." They wonder what will be there today. Sometimes they themselves bring suggestions. In an occasional school room, a committee arranges the panel each week.

The yarn spinners' club. "The Yarn Spinners' Club" or "The Paul Bunyan Club" meets for an hour on every other Thursday evening right after school. The only requisite for membership is the writing of a story. Even the teacher cannot belong unless she writes a story. The stories are read aloud at each meeting and are discussed and evaluated by the group. Each yarn spinner keeps a notebook of his stories. At the end of the year a mimeographed little book of the best stories of all the members is prepared by the group. Since the members of the group are those who enjoy writing, the club sometimes is a real literary influence.

Class development of a story from a story-telling picture. Reading the picture may include some or all of the following:

    a. Guessing what is happening in the picture.

    b. Characterizing the people and suggesting possible names for them.

    c. Deciding what events might have led up to the present action.

    d. Guessing at the various ways the story might turn out.

    e. Finding words to express the feelings and actions at which the picture hints.

    f. Finding words to describe the scenery or to express the background of the picture.

    g. Suggesting a few appropriate titles.

The teacher and the children either write their own versions of the story or write on one of the titles suggested by the class.

After children have had training in studying pictures together, it is better to have the stories written without discussion. If the child sees in the picture an experience similar to one he has had, the story will usually be a better one.

The first of the following stories, "Disobeying Mother," was written in grade 6 after a class discussion; the second, "A Happy Little Maid," was a volunteer grade-4 story on a picture on the bulletin board. Ruth's story (she was in grade 1) was written from a picture she herself painted. Her pictures are full of action and readily suggest stories.

DISOBEYING MOTHER

One day Johnny woke up and saw the golden sun shining on the ice pond in the field. "What a good day to go skating," he said. But the day was not so good as it looked for the golden sun had melted the ice, and Johnny had fallen in. The poor boy went home dripping wet and shivering with cold.

When he got home, his mother was not there. "All the better for me," he said. "I'll get my clothes dry before she comes." At once he started to build the fire and made it burn brightly. Then he took off his wet clothes and got a comforter to wrap around himself. Jip, the long-haired dog, went with him to keep him company. He sits under the stove in a crouching position. Jip is wondering what Johnny will get when she comes.

The boy is sitting there listening, and fearing what will happen when Mother comes. The water in the pail is steaming and is very hot.

As he was sitting there he heard a noise. "That must be Mother," he said. But it was too late to get away. Mother came into the room. "Why, Johnny Brown," she said. "You've turned the house upside down and you've got my new comforter, too. Now you'll get a cold."

A HAPPY LITTLE MAID

Little Ann Block was three years old. One day after her daddy had gone to the office, Ann's mother brought out some rags and a pan of water. "Ann," she said, "it is such a nice day, don't you want to go out doors?"

"No, no," said Ann, shaking her curly mop of hair.

"Then why don't you play in the nursery," said her mother. "I don't want you in my way. I am going to wash windows."

"No, no," replied Ann, shaking her head again. "Ann's going to wash windows too."

"Now, whoever gave you that idea?" asked her mother.

"Ann did," said Ann.

"You cannot wash windows," said Mrs. Block firmly, "and you know it. Please stop bothering me." But Ann kept right on teasing. Finally Mrs. Block tired of Ann's teasing. "All right," she said. "You may wash the windows in the bathroom." She got out a dishpan, four rags, and an old stool. She took them in the bathroom and watched Ann climb up on the stool, her face full of smiles.

About twelve o'clock in walked Mr. Block. "Where's my little sugar-plum?" he asked.

"She's not hiding again. Go in the bathroom and see," said his wife with a smile on her face. When Mr. Block opened the door, there stood Ann on the stool wringing out a rag.

"I'm helping Mother," she said proudly.

"So you are," laughed Mr. Block. "But come now, it's time for lunch."

RUTH'S STORY

One day Rosemary went down hill on her sled. Her brother, George, was on the back of the sled, but he fell off. He picked himself up and ran after the sled.

George said, "Rosemary, don't bump into the snowman, try to steer your sled another way." But it was too late and Rosemary went bump, bump, bump, into the snowman.

The class story book. No wonder children want to write stories for the class story book. First of all, the book itself is large and showy. The covers are of cardboard, covered with cloth or wall paper. The title is intriguing. The leaves of the book are of brown paper or newsprint which makes a nice background for pasting the children's stories. The book itself is so big that it stands half-open on the floor or lies open on a table.

The class story book belongs to all the children. It contains the best stories of each child. An author may illustrate his story if he wishes, or may ask a friend in the room to do it for him.

The principal is proud of the book. She reads the new stories when she comes into the room. All visitors read the class story book.

No child's story can be put into the book until it is written legibly and all words are spelled correctly. The sentences must be right, too. The teacher will help anyone who asks for help. She is the chief adviser. She has a committee to take care of the arrangement and pasting of the stories and pictures.

The class has a poetry book of its own, too. A great deal of writing finds its way into both books. "It is almost like seeing your story in print," said one little girl who was always opening the book to look at her story.

A story from a trip. Perhaps the class takes a trip together. Perhaps a child goes away for the week-end. He comes back having had at least one adventure. In lower grades the story may come out in "Sharing Time." In upper grades a class assignment or a "Trip Box" may help the story get told. Try to help the children to leave out the rest of the trip and to elaborate on one adventure only.

Notice how well the following simple incident is told:

THE SNAKE

On a turtle-catching trip at camp, we were rowing the boat near shore when the boy that was watching for turtles yelled, "What's that?" We all looked where he was pointing. There was a pile of grass in the water and on it there was a snake.

The sun was shining on him, and his eyes were sparkling in the sun. He was about two inches thick and about four feet long, if he had been stretched out. His brownish-red skin blended in with the weeds he was lying on. He lay there staring at us until we came up within four feet of him. Then he moved slowly into the water.

Human interest stories. The newspapers are full of little incidents or news items which are excellent "story starters." If a teacher will clip these items and file them, she will soon have enough to interest the whole class. Let each child choose from the lot the one that suggests a story to him.

Many writers of short stories and book-length novels get their ideas from news items.

The following were clipped from the Milwaukee Journal, a newspaper:

PROWLER HAS A MEAL AS HOUSEWIFE SLEEPS

Dallas, Tex. (AP)—It didn't cost many points, and besides her sleep wasn't disturbed.

Before Dawn a prowler entered Mrs. J. P. Woodward's home, went to the kitchen and cooked a meal. After eating, the prowler washed the dirty dishes, stacked them neatly on the drainboard and left.

Mrs. Woodward slept through it all.

Here is Katinka, a large White Rock, and the egg she has just laid on a velvet cushion on the davenport in the home of Mrs. John Robl in the town of Milwaukee. Katinka refuses to lay an egg in any other spot. When she feels that it is time for her to pay for the friendship her owner gives her, Katinka insists on being admitted to the house. As soon as she has made her contribution to the food supply of the home, she demands her reward, a bit of liver sausage and a leaf of lettuce. And if she doesn't get the reward promptly, she sets up such a screeching that Mrs. Robl hastens to "pay off."

HELP, POLICE, POLICE! AND WHAT A JOB
POLICE MADE OF IT

Too many policemen spoiled the capture of two twelve-year-old milk thieves Friday night at the Luick Dairy Company's south side branch at 2738 South 13th Street.

Oscar Dressler of 1222 W. Cleveland Avenue, plant watchman, surprised the boys stealing milk from a truck. He collared them and hailed a passerby, asking him to call the police. The over-enthusiastic pedestrian told police there was a hold-up at the dairy.

Police, recalling the sensational hold-up and killings at the Luick N. 6th Street plant in November, 19—, responded with two uniformed squads, a detective squad, and some motorcycle police.

Dressler was so amazed at his reinforcements that he fainted and lost his grip, and the two boys disappeared in the darkness.

LOST AUTOGRAPH BOOK BACK WITH A SINATRA

Philadelphia, Pa. (AP)—Anna Manacini has Frank Sinatra's autograph, thanks to the navy.

The 16 year old girl lost her book—filled with signatures of notables and with a blank page reserved for the swoon king's name. A navy officer found the book.

Public relations headquarters sent it to Frank Sinatra, who returned it to Anna with this note: "Best wishes. I'm glad we found your book."

An original animal story. After a number of stories centered around a point of interest have been read, children love to tell or write similar stories of their own. The stories may be true or "made-up." They may be little or very big. Here are a little one from grade 1 and a big one from grade 5:

AT THE FARM

Once when I was with my mother and father we saw a big horse. My mother said it would bite my ears, but I just laughed.

THE STORY OF WHITEFOOT

Whitefoot was a midget horse. He lived in Grand Canyon with the rest of the herd. His father was the second in command and was a little larger than the rest of the horses, but the leader was the largest.

Whitefoot's great-grandparents were put in the canyon by some Indians, who owned them, for safe keeping during an Indian war. When the Indians came to get them they found that a part of the trail had slipped down into the canyon. Because of lack of food and water the horses got very small. But their heads stayed large and they looked very funny. Whitefoot was almost a three-year-old. He had two older sisters and one younger brother.

It was very hot and there had been no water for two weeks. All their water was from the juice of the cactus growing here and there. It was afternoon when some of the horses trotted up to the shady cave which was their home. The leader with others had gone to find some wells which were not dried up. Whitefoot wished he could have gone but his father told him he was to be in command while they were away. He had always dreamed of this. Everything went fine for a few days. Then one of the colts gave a loud whinny and galloped to her mother. She said she could hear some one coming and it was a bear. Whitefoot went to find out if any others had seen it. He heard a whinny and saw a large bear about to pounce on another colt. Whitefoot lowered his head and ran at the bear. The bear clawed him. Whitefoot's hooves flashed as he struck at the bear which backed toward the cliff. Finally he pushed the bear over the edge. How happy he was. He had saved the colt. His father was so proud of him. He gave the command to Whitefoot.

Stories suggested by another story. Primary children, especially, are fired to make up stories after one has been read to them. Sometimes their tales are entirely different from the stories read, but the general idea is often much the same.

These four stories resulted in a senior kindergarten after the teacher had read "Hello, I'm Adeline" to the group. The children talked over the possibility that their toys might play while they were away, and the stories came immediately. Notice the artistic ending of the third story.

Last night I went downstairs in my pajamas. All my dollies were running around and jumping on the davenport. One jumped right into my arms and she was real all the time. Mama asked what I was doing and I said I was having fun downstairs. The dollies were real and she didn't even know it.

Marilyn was sleeping. A fairy came into the house. She got in bed with Marilyn. She was cold so the fairy pulled up the covers and then she covered me up, too.

I saw fairies praying on Debby's bed. I tiptoed up and touched their wings. They were soft like a feather. Then the fairy took us up to Heaven and there was Mary holding baby Jesus. God was there, too, and He was praying, too. Then we tiptoed away.

My Jack O'Lantern will have arms and feet, one string to make it run and one string to make it clap. I'll bring it to school and it will scare all the boys and girls and they'll run home.

Stories that come from history. If history becomes visual to children and if they become interested in historical fiction, they may want to try their hands at writing imaginary stories about people of long ago.

This diary of a pioneer child who was going by covered wagon to California was written by an eighth-grade girl in a one-room school.

May 3, 1826

Dear Diary: Today we made much headway towards our destination. Father shot a deer which will provide us with meat for awhile. We went 15 miles.

May 4, 1826

Dear Diary: Everything went well today except Sis fell from the wagon and hurt her knees. The heat was just bearable today. We traveled 20 miles.

May 5, 1826

Dear Diary: Shucks. Three days gone by, and I thought this was going to be fun and exciting. It's so hot I wish I was back home. We went 20 long miles.

May 6, 1826

Dear Diary: I take it all back what I said yesterday, Diary. We were completely surrounded by hostile Indians about noon but they went away with two of our cattle. After they went we were so shaken and scared we made only 10 miles progress.

May 7, 1826

Dear Diary: Today was terrible. One of our men was killed by Indians and 4 of our people are sick. Tonight under the light of the moon we will bury our brave man.

May 8, 1826

Dear Diary: Today was Sunday and tonight Father is going to read us a chapter from the Bible. We got 25 miles.

May 9, 1826

Dear Diary: Our 4 sick people were sent to Heaven today.

May 10, 1826

Dear Diary: Well, it happened today; our axle broke and we got 10 miles.

May 11, 1826

Dear Diary: A successful day was made and we got 20 miles more of our journey sawed off.

May 12, 1826

Dear Diary: Went 25 miles today.

May 13, 1826

Dear Diary: A baby was born today, Lucinda Ann. Went 20 miles.

May 14, 1826

Dear Diary: Sis was 10 today. Went 20 miles.

"This reminds me of—." Keep a box in your English class filled with words and phrases which might suggest stories. On slips of paper write such words or phrases as: fell flat, face like a lion, gravy, I trembled all over, my worst scare, ghost, snake, hair stood on end, a hair-raising yell, nightmare, telephone rang, and it was all over. On a rainy, dull day, let each

member of the class choose a slip and tell or write whatever story the words call to mind. If the slip the pupil drew strikes no answering bell in his mind, let him choose another.

The word "gravy" made Kirk, in the seventh grade, think of this experience:

GOOD GRAVY

Gravy is nice to eat but it isn't any fun to swim in. I did the latter when I was a young lad attending a Fourth of July picnic. I, with all the boldness and braveness of my two years, tumbled out of my buggy. As I waddled along the ground, filled with the pride of my new achievement, I paid no heed to where I was walking. When a scream burst from my mother's lips, I thought she was unduly excited about my little excursion. And then *it* happened. I landed "ker-plunk" right in the middle of a large kettle filled to the brim with nice, warm, appetizing gravy. Realizing at once that this was something to be excited over, I let out a wail that stopped my mother dead in her tracks, but only for a moment. In another second she had lifted me out of my potential bathtub and was telling me how lucky I was not to be burned. My clean, white clothes were covered with a thick coating of brown gravy. That's why I must give you this warning. When you want a bath, use water—not gravy.

Guessing stories from book covers. A second grade teacher of my acquaintance was lucky enough to get some colorful book covers from the city library. She wanted to make a bulletin board to advertise Book Week. Before she used the covers, she got a bright idea: Why not show the covers to the children and let them make up stories before they read the books?

Her second-grade pupils were delighted. They studied the covers, and many volunteered stories. Later she read the books to the children. She was astonished to find that they liked their own stories best.

Two of the children's stories follow. Notice how the second story is written.

THE POKY LITTLE PUPPY

Once I saw a puppy. He was very poky. When boys and girls told him to run he would hop like a rabbit, so now the boys and girls call him the poky little puppy. He is white and brown and has a tail that curls us like a doughnut. He loves to play outdoors. He is a playful little puppy. I like him very much.

I see a little puppy. He looks happy. He is without worries. I think he is sniffing at something. Can you guess who he is?

THE NEW PET

Betty was lonesome. She was looking out of the window. She saw a little rabbit. She asked her daddy to catch it. Her father went to the garage and got a net. He went very softly behind the rabbit. He put the net suddenly over the rabbit. Then he took the rabbit to Betty. Betty was happy. The rabbit was very scared at first. When he was there a few days he was very naughty. So Betty had to let the rabbit go. She was sad, very sad. Oh, yes, she was sad. So her daddy had to get her a dog. The dog was scared too. He was very, very good at first. Then he was so naughty. Betty had to let him go too. Oh! oh! She was so sad. She began to cry. Her daddy had to buy a cat. The cat was very, very naughty. So they had to give him away. Betty was so, so sad. She got a goldfish. The goldfish got out of his bowl all the time. So they gave him away too. Betty said, "Uncle is coming. He will have to be my pet." Betty went to the window. She said, "Here he comes now. Is he really in the Army? Oh, oh, oh, I am so glad. You are my pet." It was a few days after Betty's uncle had to go back to the Army. Just when he went back he gave Betty a canary. The canary always woke Betty and her father and mother up. One day the canary was not in his cage. Betty looked all over but he was not in the house. So if he got outside he would fly away. One day Betty's mother got a baby. Betty said that the baby was the best pet of all.

Nature stories. On a hike in the snow, one discovers many stories written in the animal tracks. Here a dog chased a rabbit, and there two squirrels played a brisk game of tag. Children enjoy elaborating on these stories when they return from the hike.

If the teacher has led each child to keep his eyes open to the happenings going on all about him, little stories like the following will find their way into the story box. Children should be encouraged to write about little happenings. Carol saw this robin story enacted just outside her father's store window.

A FOXY WORM

We think a robin is very ordinary, but did you ever stop and watch one for awhile? I did. I looked out of our store window and saw two robins. They were looking for worms. The bigger robin went ahead and cocked his head to one side, for you know they listen for worms, and thought he had one, but didn't. He cocked his head again and this time had one. The other robin saw the worm and tried to get it. While they were arguing, the worm must have gotten away because one robin looked down and flew away. The other robin did the same thing. The foxy worm got the best that time.

Autobiographies. Children should be encouraged to write their autobiographies. Such stories not only are interesting to write and read, but give the teacher much insight into the child's background of experience.

Autobiographies usually prove to be more interesting if they are written as a series of episodes in the life of a child rather than as a running tale. Such a plan as this might be worked out in class together. Some appropriate topics may be suggested by the following phrases:

My earliest memory.	I was so embarrassed.
My best (or my first) friend.	I was all mixed up.
My first day at school.	My happiest day.
The one I loved most.	When I was sick.
My first trip.	The pet I love.
My new dress.	

If the teacher writes her autobiography too, the children will be more interested in writing theirs. The class writer might take an episode from each child's life and weave them together into a class story about an imaginary class member. These two episodes from fifth-grade autobiographies are typical. These children made their autobiographies for their mothers.

MY PET

It was the year of 19— that I had a pet. It was a dog. We named it Pal, with the help of our neighbors. Pal was tannish brown with a white chest and a white foot. He had big brown eyes. Even from far away you could tell he had a loving look in them.

Pal knew many tricks. He could dance, shake hands, and stay where you told him to. Pal would follow me wherever I went.

He was getting to be a big dog, so we couldn't keep him in the city.

The day he was to be taken to my grandmother's I will never forget. My father, brother, sister, and I were doing the dishes. My mother was sitting on a chair beside the stove. Pal was sitting and watching us do the dishes. All of a sudden my mother burst into tears. It had been hard for me to choke down my sobs before, but now, try as I might, tears came. Pal went to Mamma and put his paws on her knees. Then they both cried together. What a sight! Now my tears flowed freely. I will never as long as I live forget that day.

THE JOKE'S ON ME

Say, do you like bones?

Well, one day we went to my aunt and uncle's for April Fool's Day. My uncle came out with a box of candy—at least it looked like one. I started to open it. Then when I got through opening ten pieces of paper I peeked in the box. What in the world do you think was there? More paper yet. I started to unwrap piece by piece until I got five more unwrapped. There in the box was a bone, a big one too. Then their dog Impy came and begged for the bone. I gave it to him. He and the cat Snooks went walking away as if they had a thousand dollars.

Script for radio stories. Sometimes radio stations will allow schools (both rural and city) to have free time on Friday mornings to present programs over the air. These programs consist of original stories and plays which the children have made up—usually around a common theme. This type of program is a powerful incentive for original work.

If a school has no opportunity to broadcast over a real radio, it can have fun with a "mike" in school programs.

Script for original comic strips. There is no doubt that children love funny papers and comic strips. Since this is so (and there can be no denying it), why not capitalize on its good points?

In almost every room there is a child who can draw well. Why not arrange for this child to draw an episode for an original comic strip once every week? Since artists some-times lack ideas of their own, why not form a three-man syndicate—one to furnish the ideas, one to draw the episode, and one to write a running story under the picture?

This not only will give the room one more activity of which to be proud, but might furnish three young chaps—none too fond of school, perhaps—with a profitable enter-prise.

Stories from titles. For many years, teachers in junior high schools have suggested stories to their pupils by putting lists of story titles on the board. However, intermediate teachers have not made enough use of this device. It is well to include a number of titles in the list, since one or two may not be enough to challenge the entire class. The children will usually write about the title which brings one of their own experi-ences to mind. The next two stories from grade 6 are true.

HAIR-RAISER

The windmill spun vigorously in the smart morning breeze. Two boys walked out of their house and down to the boat docks, where a tender was awaiting them. After getting their boat "Popo" ready, they soon found themselves attached to a long line of boats which were destined for the race. A small boat towed them out to the starting point.

As the sailors were cast free from the tow boat, a brisk wind sprang up. The sails wiggled and flapped madly. In a little while, everything was ready for the big event. Popo leaped forward with the rest. It seemed as though each boat tried to get to the buoy first.

A man was standing on the deck of the judges' boat shouting instructions to all the skippers as they sailed past. Now Popo's turn came. As she sped by, a wave swept them out of hearing distance. Thinking the message unimportant, they resumed their course. All of a sudden a baby squall was born. The wind covered the lake like a blanket. A shot was fired from the judges' boat. These sailors thought it was the starting gun. They urged Popo onward. After a period of five minutes, they glanced around and saw no sign of the other boats.

About this time, one of them noticed a small hole forming in the sail—it seemed to grow larger with every gust. This was not their only trouble, for quick as a flash Popo was being swept across the lake, helplessly in danger of striking the rocks.

On shore, a police boat weighed anchor and came to the rescue. Popo was pulled back to safety at the end of a nice, long painter.

If you don't think these boys had a nightmare after that experience, just try it sometime!

A MIDNIGHT VISITOR

It was about 8:00 at night. Mother and Dad had just left the house to go to a party. I was all alone. I was listening to the radio and I decided to read. When the clock struck 12:00, I decided to go to bed. I had just gotten into bed when I thought I heard a knock at the door. I started to get up. Then the knock came louder. I said, "All right, I'm coming." I got down there but no one was there. I went back in bed and then I heard a voice say, "Put your hands up and keep them up!" I did. Pretty soon I heard footsteps on the stairs. I was frightened. The door opened and I heard some one laughing. I turned around and there stood father. He asked me what I was doing and I told him what had happened. Then he really laughed. "Why, you left the radio turned on and what you heard was a midnight mystery story."

First-sentence starters. Several English books suggest first sentences or paragraphs for children to develop into complete stories.

If a teacher is not clever at composing these "story-starters," she can copy first sentences from library books and short stories written for the grade level of the children she is teaching. Such paragraphs as these are typical:

John stood stock still. His legs refused to go. The sweat broke out on his forehead.

"She's gone! Now I am going to find her diary," muttered John to himself as he crept up the stairs noiselessly.

Writing endings to stories. You have almost finished reading an exciting tale to your class. Before the children find out how it actually turns out, let each write the ending the way he would like it. Sometimes the children's ideas are better than the author's.

Stories from a character described. Show the children the picture of a person, and together try to find out what story might happen to such a chap.

This story was suggested by the picture of Mr. Brown asleep under a tree with a pheasant coming from behind.

OLD MR. BROWN AND HIS HUNTING TRIP

It was a warm autumn afternoon when Mr. Brown dressed in has shabby hunting clothes, took his dog and gun, and walked down to his 60 acres of woodland. He and his dog crawled through the barb-wire fence. He walked for about two hours when his bones got tired. He and his dog sat all hunched up under an oak tree. As he watched the clouds floating in the robin's egg blue sky he scratched his mustache and then suddenly remembered it was Mrs. Brown's birthday and he was supposed to catch her a pheasant for supper. Well, company was coming from far away up north, for supper. As he and his dog, "Cocoa Spot," were sitting by the oak, he visualized himself after the pheasant he was supposed to get. It was getting hot and stuffy, and he was getting drowsy. As his eyes closed a happy and kind-hearted look crept over his face. As soon as his eyes closed who should appear but the forgotten pheasant. He stood there, ruffled his feathers, and made a peculiar sound. The sun was setting. Time flew on and on until it was five or six o'clock. The clouds white and fluffy were now gradually turning light pink and blue. Time crept on but Mr. Brown slept on and the pheasant slipped daintily away into the woods, and Mr. Brown never saw him again.

Stories for sheer fun. Can't you just imagine what fun these fifth-grade children had, seeing what "whoppers" they could tell?

THE LIVING-ROOM HOTEL

We went away one Sunday afternoon and anything could happen. When we came home, there was a bird's nest on the table lamp and four eggs in it.

You see, we left the window open, so we left the eggs in my bedroom. When they hatched, they packed their bags and went.

(Edward, who wrote this, has real style to his writing.)

SOME LUCK

It all happened when I was living in a rustic little cabin by Liar's Lake. One bright sunny morning as I was out fishing near the forested shore I saw a huge 32 point buck deer that hunters had been trying to shoot for years. I was so excited I hopped madly up and down. This tipped my creaky old boat over, and I naturally fell into the lake. I came up with my limit of bass, bluegills, croppies, sunfish, and one huge pike in my boots.

I rowed back to my cabin after righting my boat, and as I had enough fish I decided to go snipe hunting. I loaded my rifle and my trusty old double barrel shotgun, and rowed across the serene little lake. I cocked both of my guns, and leaned them against the quaint seat of the boat.

Suddenly a ten-pound snipe ran out from behind a tree. I fired my rifle and missed the snipe. At that moment, the 32-point buck I had seen earlier in the day ran out of the woods and my rifle killed him. He fell in my boat and the jar set off my shotgun, and a dozen fat ducks fell in my boat.

I rowed wearily back to my cabin and unloaded my game. As I was doing this I heard my telephone ring. I had won one thousand dollars from the Pot-o'-Gold program. Some luck!

Stories centering around a place described. Perhaps the paragraph you are reading to your pupils is a description of a haunted house, a foreign palace or a tumbledown hut. When you have finished reading, ask each pupil to imagine a story that might happen in such a place.

Perhaps you are not reading the description but are showing the children a picture of an interesting-looking place. Either procedure should net some good stories, especially if your group is used to writing.

Type stories. Kipling's "Just So Stories," especially the one about how the elephant's child got his long trunk, delight the heart of any intermediate child.

It is a short step from the "Just So Stories" to the children's imagining how some other things got to be. These two fifth-grade stories give you two children's ideas.

HOW THE SKUNK GOT HIS STRIPES

Many years ago, probably a million, there was a family of skunks. Now they were a pretty bunch of skunks as skunks go. Peter was the youngest of them and, being the baby, of course he was rather spoiled. Well, now, Mrs. Skunk was a very nice woman and a very religious animal. Each Sunday she insisted on her four snow-white children going to Sunday school. Skunks were white then. Peter thought that going to Sunday school was silly. So each Sunday he would go to the edge of the east part of the forest where they lived and roll and roll in the black, watery dirt that was near the edge of the swimming hole.

Poor Mrs. Skunk did everything she could think of to punish Peter but nothing helped. At last she went to the fairy that lived near-by in a hollow log. She was a good fairy and listened to Mrs. Skunk tell her story. The fairy said that she would try to teach Peter a lesson. The next Sunday Peter tried his old trick again. When his mother was scrubbing him, which he liked very much, a funny thing happened. The more his mother rubbed, the blacker he got except for one stripe down the middle of his back. That became white again. Poor Peter surely felt terrible but to this day the skunk must bear the shame Peter brought by being black and white instead of snow white.

HOW THE WATER HOSE CAME TO BE

Way back in prehistoric times when big animals killed all the smaller ones, there was a little beaver named Paddy. Every day little Paddy crawled up along the bank of the river in search of food. There was one particular path in which he liked to walk better than any of the others. In this path a daisy grew. Strangely enough, this flower had not any leaves on it. Years and years passed and the little daisy was still there but the stem had become hollow and turned white. Bugs had drilled holes in the top of the flower. Spring came and the little beavers were blowing bubbles in a little stream near-by. Suddenly some one blew some water into a hole in the ground and it came out of the daisy. That was the first water hose.

Stories from books children like. If you have finished reading a book the children like, let them imagine another episode that the author didn't tell. The boys could think, for instance, of another scrape Tom Sawyer could have gotten into. (It probably will sound strangely like an experience of theirs.) This story should not be in the nature of an assignment, but will interest a few volunteers.

Characters children create. One of your children, in a story he writes for class, may one day create a character that is a real story personage. If so urged, the author or one of the other children might be interested in writing further stories about the character. The story collection might eventually form a book. This type of writing has great possibilities for a few children who greatly like to write.

Stories about pets. Children are anxious to tell about their pets. Such stories are among their best contributions. You can guess why. Notice the imaginative touch in the first story (grade 5) and the word pictures in the second (grade 7).

PINKY

Pinky is a little chicken. The reason I call her Pinky is because I got her for Easter. When daddy brought her home, she was colored pink. You know how pets are colored sometimes.

By some way, which I don't remember, we got the color off so she looked natural at last.

We tried to housebreak Pinky and she learned.

A few weeks after we got her, she was climbing on the davenport. She fell off and almost broke her leg. I patched her up and then she was as good as new.

When Pinky was a young lady, she met a rooster. We finally had to buy the rooster because we got tired of going out in the field every night looking for her and the rooster. You know these teen-age girls. She finally got married after we looked all over this side of the globe for a chicken preacher.

When Pinky was all grown up she laid her eggs on the softest pillow in the house.

We've still got Pinky and you can come to see her anytime.

MY PET

A friend and I were playing "Monopoly" on the floor (I was too lazy to get the card table out) when my dog, Pal, came running in. She was coming full speed and slid on the rug and right into the "Monopoly" game, like a baseball player does when he's sliding home. The money went flying like advertisements do when the pilot drops them from an airplane.

She looked rather ridiculous, her front paws spread out straight and her back paws bent under her. She looked surprised and so did we. Her big brown eyes shone, and so did her black coat. Her ears were flopping and her tail was wagging. After her sudden stop, she just stood there and looked at us with a cocked head. Then she tried to swallow one of the dice.

It took half an hour to clean up the mess and all Pal did was to lie on the rug and grin at us as if it were a joke.

Stories for special days. This title is self-explanatory. How do you like Shirley's Hallowe'en story and Bob's story (grade 8) for "Be Kind to Animals" Week?

HALLOWE'EN

"Boo!" cried Jimmy.

It was Hallowe'en night and Mary was having a Hallowe'en party.

They all had on different clothes. Some were dressed like witches, others like cats, while some were like pumpkins.

When they got inside of Mary's house they were scared. They saw some big white eyes.

All of them stood still and watched them come closer and closer. When they were almost up to them they ran toward the door. But when they got to the door it was locked.

And, oh, how frightened the children were. When they came close to them again, they saw it was little Jimmy. And he frightened the children. How surprised they were.

They then ate their supper, without being afraid.

IT CAN'T RAIN FOREVER

Joey sat on the curb in front of his home. He was crying. He was wondering how anything could be so awful. Why was he crying? Well, gosh, it even hurt to think about it. Two nights ago he had just come home from school when a tall, grave looking officer had strode over to him. The officer inquired, "Are you Joey Nelson?" Joey said he was and wondered what was the trouble. Then it swept over him like a terrible storm. The man informed him sadly that a dog he was positive belonged to Joey had gotten run over and killed. Joey couldn't believe it was his dog. He called and whistled for his pet but no friendly bark came. Those sparkling eyes were gone forever.

This is why Joey was sitting on the curb sobbing. It was like he had lost his last friend. Still he couldn't believe it. He called and clapped his hands but nothing happened. Well, it was time for supper now and he walked, heartbroken, into the house. They were in the midst of the evening meal when a joyful "Yipe" sounded at the back door. Small paws scratched furiously at the screen. Joey got up from his chair, upsetting his milk and bumping the table violently. The happy dog dashed in and Joey hugged him tightly. The policeman had been mistaken.

A dog of similar type had been killed. Just a short story reminder—be careful and drive cautiously and keep the kids happy.

Real adventures. Real adventures make good stories. Many children who do not have much imagination can tell an exciting story of a real happening.

But when exciting things happen to boys with imagination, we get stories like these (grades 5 and 7).

A RUNAWAY RAFT

My raft was tied in my cove when a storm came up. The rope broke and Hugo, our gardener, tried to get it. He got wet and let it go and then he put the rope remains on the shore. Later a paper boy asked me if I knew where my raft was and also asked me if I wanted it any more. I said it was in my cove and I wanted it. He said, "Well, she's floating round the bend."

"Yipes!" I yelled and dashed to the place where it was. I saw the last of it until after supper when we went across the river and spotted it.

Howie yelled, "There she is," and we ran back to the car to get some rope. A man took us out in his boat and we got the raft. It is now safe in the man's cove. I hope to get it after the storm is over.

P.S. Leastways, I hope I will.

SAILING, SAILING

You have all heard of the three men that went to the sea in a tub. Well, Tom and I went to sea in a trailer.

We were out to the lake one day when my dad came out with the boat on the trailer. Having a streak of the devil in us, we hid in a tree until the men were out of sight in the boat. Then we climbed down and sat on the trailer trying to think of something we shouldn't do so we could do it. We're the only two guys in the world who can produce lightning from a brainstorm. Then an idea somehow forced its way into our heads to take a ride in the trailer. So we did. A little shove was all we needed and we were on our way. How were we going to stop? That was the only flaw in our plan, only we didn't know it at the time.

Our speed increased and then we hit the water. We were all set to walk off on the tongue when we noticed to our sorrow that it was under water and the rest was sinking fast.

The water rose to our ankles, then to our knees and finally stopped. We looked at each other in dismay. We pulled the trailer back up and tried to dry it out. But we couldn't resist the temptation. We took off our shoes and did it again. What happened when we got home, outsiders will never know.

Must life soon clip their shining wings
When Care and Worry find them?
Must they like the sheep of the little Bo Peep
Leave all of their tales behind them?

Chapter V

Is the Better Bitter?

Only adults have that silly trick

Of always using a measuring stick

While children know well

When a task is done,

"Was it or wasn't it any fun?"

Chapter V

Is the Better Bitter?

LORRAINE is a sixth-grade girl in the upper room of a two-room school. She is a good student, but has no extraordinary ability. By nature she is quiet and appreciative. She loves to write and to draw.

A teacher, visiting Lorraine's class room one morning, admired the border above the blackboard. It was a fresh, charming border, eloquent of spring. Beneath a blue sky and against a background of fresh green, little spring scenes were being enacted. A butterfly lingered over a clump of flowers; a new calf investigated a family of baby chicks out walking with their mother; birds flew from the branches of a blossoming tree.

As she left the room, the visitor remarked to the children, "I certainly like the border you have made. It seems to me to have several poems in it. What is the calf thinking as it sees chickens for the first time? What is the mother hen telling her chickens about the calf? What are the bees saying to the flowers? What are the robins singing about? If any one of you finds one of the poems in the border, be sure to write it down before it gets away." She then walked out and forgot all about the incident.

Lorraine, however, did not forget. When the visiting teacher came again, Lorraine had a poem ready for her. Since you have met Lorraine, via this introduction, perhaps you would like to read her poem. I will later evaluate it as Lorraine's poem. Here it is, just as Lorraine handed it to her new friend.

SPRING

(1) Spring always makes me feel so glad
(2) So many things to see
(3) My friend the robin
(4) Greets me with his melody;
(5) And then there is the funny one,
(6) The wobbly baby calf,
(7) He stands, he falls, he tries again,
(8) He sure does make me laugh.
(9) There also is the mother hen
(10) Scolding her chicks—
(11) They got out of the pen.
(12) Then there is the butterfly
(13) So very pretty and bright
(14) I think that on that flower
(15) He will again alight.
(16) We can hear the little grass talking.
(17) One said, "Shall we go walking?
(18) How do you feel about Spring?"

Evaluation of a child's poem. A child's poem should be evaluated from two points of view: (1) to determine its merits and defects; (2) to encourage the child to continue writing.

The points to be considered from the first standpoint are: honesty; originality or freshness of style, thought, form, or words; form; rhythm; and simplicity. Let us evaluate *Spring* as a child's poem.

Is there honesty? This child definitely has something to say and says it. The poem rings true. Lorraine was not just trying to write a poem.

Is there originality or freshness of style, thought, form, or words? This poem has a little different treatment of the subject than is usual in a spring poem. She seems actually to be seeing the scenes she tells about. She has not made a parody or tried to copy the style of another poem.

Lorraine does not use many trite words and expressions in her verse. The following phrases are artistic: feel so glad; my friend the robin greets me; wobbly baby calf; little grass talking. Her best picture is the line about the baby calf—"He stands, he falls, he tries again." Her last line is artistic; it rounds out the poem. We can see the word pictures and hear the tone pictures in Lorraine's poem. Later, as she continues to write, a teacher can help Lorraine to find better transitory words than the *then* she frequently uses in starting a new thought. But right now the only interests of a teacher of creative writing should be to keep Lorraine writing poetry and to awaken in her many avenues of thought.

How is the form? The form of Lorraine's poem matches the lightness of the verse; it is not stiff or formal. The style changes in the last three lines.

How is the rhythm? This poem has rhythm flowing through it, but it does not have a definite rhyme scheme. At first glance it seems to have, but lines 9 to 11 convince the reader that this poet knows nothing of verse-making. As you re-read the poem aloud, you will feel flaws in the even flow of the lines. As Lorraine reads more poetry, and listens to poetry read aloud, her sensitive ear will discover the difference between a smooth line and an uneven one. Until her ears hears the difference, it will be of little use to point out the defect in her work to her. Such attention to form may destroy her spontaneity.

To a child, poetry is something to get out of the system; not a thing to polish after he has written it. He is appalled that he wrote a verse, and to him his verse is good. If he must perfect the form, his spontaneous joy in achievement is gone, and a poem is only work—and school work at that.

Is there simplicity? This poem is guilty of no wordiness. It is simply written. The word *surely* would be more artistic than *sure does* in the line about the calf.

Spring is a typical child's poem. The treatment is better than the average, but the flaws are the usual childish ones. When children's poems reach a length of more than four lines, they are seldom without flaws unless the writer has sacrificed meaning to form. After four lines, a child's natural sense of balance begins to run out and he strains to get balance. As a result, his verse is labored.

The evaluation made to the child. The words of the visiting teacher to whom Lorraine gave her poem follow:

"I know you are wondering what I told Lorraine about her poem. Personally, I think she has written a fine poem for a sixth-grade child whose only influence from poetry comes at school. It is the genuine expression of genuine feeling, and I liked it. Some of the thoughts are lovely. I would tell Lorraine how much I liked the poem—in fact, I did just that. I shall not tell her yet about any of the flaws in her verse. I do not believe that children should have the weak spots in their poems pointed out to them until they begin to feel the weaknesses themselves and to ask for help. Use a positive approach; point out to them the lines you especially liked because they were like music or because they made good pictures. I did this for Lorraine, and she was grateful. I have not known her well enough so that she has come to me to help her with her poetry. Until she does, I shall never point out to her the weaknesses in her poem *Spring*. Her natural mistakes are quite immaterial now because Lorraine is still a poet and not yet skilled in verse-making. This is apparent in that her poem loses its line balance after it goes on for a few lines.

"But Lorraine sees things with a poet's sensitive spirit; I intend to keep her interested in writing if I can, and I intend to know her better. The last poem she handed me had no merit in it at all. I intend to say to her when I see her next, 'That last poem didn't come up to your usual high standard, Lorraine. I believe it was because you were just trying to write. When you wait until you have something real to say, you write beautifully.' I am hoping to challenge Lorraine's verse-making without making her self-conscious.

"If and when she comes to me for help, I plan to take this poem of hers entitled *Spring* and show her where the weak spots lie. I shall choose an old poem because she will have ceased to be sensitive about it, whereas she may be sensitive about a current poem. Her coming to me of her own accord will tell me that she now is ready to be a craftsman as well as a poet.

"First I shall have Lorraine read the poem aloud to me. She will then hear what is wrong with it because she has a sensitive ear. If she doesn't hear the break in the rhythm, I shall know that she is not yet ready for a lesson in verse-making, and I shall drop the matter until a later time. However, if she does hear the flaws, I shall try to lead her to see the cause and to point out how they can be remedied. I shall not lead for any particular words because this is her poem, not mine. I believe she will notice when the line is too full and when it is too lean. I shall ask her to notice her rhyme scheme and later at home to see what she can do to improve the part of her verse which tells about the chicks. I shall not suggest a single line or word, or lead for any definite ones. I am not trying to make an exquisite gem of Lorraine's poem. I am trying to improve her technique because she is getting to the point of development where she needs a few techniques. It is her next poem I am hoping to improve, not this one. If I hope to improve her writing, I must not make her form-conscious."

Looking over the shoulders of a whole class. The following nine poems and two stories were handed in by the eleven children in a sixth-grade class of a two-teacher school at the edge of a city. These children range from high to low in ability and have attempted poetry writing since the first grade. Teachers beginning a creative program may be interested in seeing all of the contributions of a class, not just the best ones.

The idea sheet printed in Chapter III was the assignment, and no vocabulary work was done beforehand. The children had been working on a unit in air transportation for several weeks and were wildly enthusiastic about the subject, especially the boys.

Notice the freedom of expression in all the contributions, even in those of the weakest writers.

I WONDER (*by* BUDDY)

My first flying trip,
I wonder how high I'll be
How many things I'll see.
I wonder if I'll be soaring around the town,
I wonder if when I dive, I'll hit the ground.
Will I get those spells my buddy did?
What will happen to me?
Gee!

Buddy's verse has one essential of a poem—imagination. From there one can go anywhere. He has the beginning of a sense of balance. Can you feel it?

MY FIRST REAL FLIGHT (*by* EUNICE)

I am flying like a kite,
Oh; what a wonderful sight.
Not in day but at night
When the stars are twinkling bright,

I feel just like a bird
That first began to fly
Way up in the sky.
This is my first real flight
That I am taking tonight.

These three lines have the beginning feel of verse.

Encourage such writers as Eunice. Their verses may not improve particularly, but writing improves them as people.

WILL I GO?

(by LORRAINE, who wrote *Spring)*

I am now to take my first solo flight,
But it makes me chilly to think of such
    height.   } Imagination here.
What if I should crash to the ground
And never again hear a motor sound?

I know the plane will not fall apart
Because once before I saw it dart
Right above me with such terrible speed
So that I looked like a little seed   } Sense sacrificed to rhyme.
But I still will go
If I'll safely land I don't know

I will take along my parachute
But I sort of wish I was at home playing my
    flute   } Note the whimsy in these lines.
Instead of in this flying suit.

THE BIRD   *(by* JANE)

The sky is such a deep, deep blue,
A robin flew past my head,
His breast was red.   } She really sees this sky and the bird.
His coat was brown.
Do you know I had to frown.   } Just for rhyme.
I wonder what he thinks he is
He reminds me of an airplane so high in the sky. } Imaginative.
Oh, here comes a navy bomber.
It looks like that bird   } More natural and, therefore, b e t t e r verse.
He is a pretty bird.

Talk to the Janes about attempting poetry that doesn't rhyme.

(by CHARLYNE)

Up in the sky I see many birds
Big ones, little ones, but there is a big one.

It's bigger than the rest.
It has two wings like the rest, but it makes a funny noise.
Quite like a cat purring.

The last line is delightful. This child is beginning to see with a poet's eyes. Notice the brevity and spontaneity of the verse.

(by MARY)

Up in the sky so high
I can almost touch the moon
I can see the little town below
It says, "I'm not so little down below."
The night is on its way so I must say
"So long" to the little town below
I must be on my way.
So long, little town.

Mary has written a choice bit of verse. She has genuine feeling and a light hand with words. Keep Mary interested in writing.

(by DALE)

In an airplane in the sky
I like to fly, up, up, up.
But when I go up so high
My pilot makes me go down.
Some day I'm going to fly to the sun
There I'm going to have lots of fun,
Then I'm going to the moon,
Then I'll go back to the earth pretty soon
Then, I'll fly, fly, fly,
By the moon, stars and sun
There's where I have all my fun.

Dale is having lots of fun in this poem. He is actually off to the moon, and that is what we wanted, wasn't it?

(by DICK)

Up in the clouds so high
So quiet and peaceful
The sound of the quiet motors as we go along,

The sunset is so round and full and the sky
So dark and still.
That's when the air is peaceful.

Dick has quiet power in these simple lines. He has given us a feeling of largeness and peace and relaxation.

(No name)

Flying in the sky to see the world round
I went into a dive and almost hit the ground
But I was up and away like a flash and a light.

This child wrote only a few lines, but there is a real beginning here. Notice the action in the last line when he begins to forget about form. The last two boys wrote stories instead of poems.

MY FIRST SOLO   *(by* Junior*)*

Here I go! I hope I miss that tree. Oh, I just missed it. Here I am up so high. Oh what's that coming? Maybe it's a Jap plane coming after me. I wish Major Bong was with me. No, it was just a bird. It feels like I am going to fall out. Oh, I forgot to tie my safety belt on. I'd better do it now. I may as well go down. Well, here goes. Boy, is it scary. I wish that tree wasn't there. Wow! I made a good landing.

It is a privilege to hear a boy talking inside his own mind.

THE LIFE OF AN AIRPLANE   *(by* Dale*)*

I was there in a big building. There were many noises and people around me. See those men over there. They are putting another arm on me. Gee, oh gee, soon in a few weeks, I will be ready for my first flight. Now it is the last day and the people are all around me. Here comes the machine to take me out to the field.

Oh, look, here come my crew. There are the pilot and the gunners, and the radio man, too. Oh what are those they are putting into my body? They look like big watermelons with sails.

Oh, listen, oh, listen, to my heart throbbing. Now I am racing down the field. I will be flying along now for hours. So

we will soon come to the enemy country. Oh, look, there is a
flight of Jap planes. They will fill me full of holes. Gunners, let
them have it. Oh, there go my bombs now. I think I will head
for home.

Oh, boy, we shot down ten planes out of sixteen. Oh, look,
they are heading back, these fighters. Just think, four hours of
flying and I will be home. We have been flying three and one-
half hours now. I can see the field now. Well, the flight is over.

Dale lives in a world of airplanes and imaginary flights.
I can imagine how his paper flight released him. I like the
line, "Oh, listen, oh, listen to my heart throbbing."

Thumbnail comments on children's verse. The poems in
the next group are interesting.

TWO DEER

I saw two deer out in the field,
And when they saw me
They turned and wheeled.
Off in the woods they ran,
And I never saw the two deer again.

A grade-6 Indian boy wrote this. It is one of the finest
examples of simplicity that I have ever found. The more you
read it, the more it seems to mean. The boy is a true poet.
We have a feeling as we read his last line that there is much
in the poem which is not said.

IN THE MOONLIGHT

The bundles of cornstalks standing in fields
Look like Indian tepees
By the light of the moon.
And the little rabbits running to and fro
Are the Indian boys
We would like to know.

Nancy is always writing. She is advanced for her grade,
which is the second, and writing keeps her interested. She
likes to make comparisons.

Out in the country one October morning
I saw colored trees with red, orange, and yellow leaves.
I saw a pheasant in the cornfield
Where shocks stood with pumpkins lying around them.
In the nearby woods I saw a squirrel running up and
    down the trees.
As the morning went on the animals and birds seemed
    to vanish
And just the scene remained.

Dallas has caught the real spirit of a still fall day in this word picture. His last two lines would do credit to a mature writer.

MY LITTLE SAIL BOAT

I whittled me a little boat
Of firewood strong and broad.
It flowed down a little stream
And down a little brook.
The boat was very happy,
Which was very plain to see,
To float along so free and strong
With no one there to stop it.

Letty, in grade 6, has rhythm. You can feel this brook flow even without rhyme. When Letty becomes aware of rhyme, she will write even better poetry because you feel the rhyme trying to come out in these lines, but it doesn't quite make it.

Darwin, grade eight, has a highly developed word sense. He both writes well and draws well. His poem shows that he is a verse-maker, as well as a poet, and that he is a mature lad.

THE LOST FRIEND

Near a rock
On a hill
Where the river
Takes a spill,
An autumn wind
Laid it down

An orphan seed
Upon the ground.
Came the snow
Came the cold
Lay the seed
Beneath its fold.

Dreary months
All the same
Then with the sun
A new spring came.
More winters passed
Each spring, a fall
The tree branched out
Grew straight and tall.
But now
It shades no native sod
It's gone
And by the will of God,
No more
To stand so dark and high
To silhouette
Against the sky.
The river runs
And takes its spill
Near rock and stump
Upon a hill.
But never more
The tree stands high
Its branches
Brushing clear the sky.
The rays of heat
Which pierced the snow

Started rivulets
To flow.
In rich black earth
The seed took hold
A mighty tree
Began to mold.
Through fresh spring rain
And burning sun
The little seed
Its life begun.
Again the fall
Again the snow
And still the tree
Stayed on to grow.
For it has long
Been cut away
It now stands as a cross
So gray.
It now stands guard
By a lonely hill,
No river runs
Or takes its spill.
But that autumn wind
Has found its friend
An orphan seed
Near a river's bend.

Encourage your children to see the unusual in the usual. That is what Marilyn, who is in the sixth grade, has done so well in the following poem:

JACK FROST

Jack Frost is here,
It's getting colder.
Some of his pictures are on my windows.
He lets me look in his big folder,
And pick out the picture I want.

Three more poems by young children, the ideas for which were suggested by natural events, follow:

THE RAIN DROPS

Drip, drop, drip, drop,
The rain goes "Plop!"
Drip, drop, drip, drop,
Goes the splashing lot.
It goes slapping against the house.
The shiny little needles go
Drip, drop, drip, drop,
The needles go slapping as they like
Flapping go the little splashing rain drops,
Drip, drop, drip, drop.

Courtney, in grade 4, has listened to the rain and caught
its monotonous sound. If you can teach your children to
listen, they too can write. To listen is to write.

LEAVES

See the leaves twisting downward
Twirling, twisting as they go.
See the leaves go twirling downward
Trying to make their colors show.

A little different idea of why leaves twirl as they fall. If
children are interested, they will tell you what they see. Brice
is not always interested in school work. He has a fine mind,
but seems often to live in a world of his own thoughts. This
poem is his *first* attempt at creative writing. If a child of this
type in the seventh grade can find expression in creativity of
some sort, he will leave his world of dreams.

OLD JACK FROST

Old Jack Frost,
It's fall now,
Time to get up and work.
Rest is over, it's time
To have fun.
Old man Winter is waiting,
Next summer you can rest again.

The last poem also was written by a child in the fourth grade.

ON A TOBOGGAN SLIDE

It was a cold but clear winter day.
The sun was shining on the frosted snow.
I was trying to think of a place to go.
"To the toboggan slide, that's the place to play!"
I took my sled and was on my way
To the top of the toboggan slide I climbed
Laid down on my sled
Not looking to see if anyone was ahead.
As I was going down, I heard a cry—
"Look out!" that seemed to come from the clear blue sky.
But it was too late—
My sled tipped and I went rolling in the snow.
I sat there, looking at the man
I had hit a moment ago.
Soon up he rose
Brushed off his clothes
Then slowly he came over by my side.
He said, "Lad, I guess to both of us it was a surprise."
Not knowing what to say,
I just picked up my sled
And said, "Next time I go down this tobaggan slide
I'll remember to look ahead."

Gale, better known as Buddy to his friends, wrote this poem about his experience on a new toboggan slide which the city had provided for the young people. He was in the seventh grade.

When children write of true experiences, their verse usually is more "jingley" than poetic. Notice how Buddy has avoided this for the most part.

In order to get adolescents to realize what natural things change and growth are, it is well sometimes to think with them about the beliefs they have outgrown. The following poem by a seventh-grade pupil is typical.

WHEN I WAS LITTLE I THOUGHT—

When I was small I thought
The rainbow was a gateway to Heaven.
I thought rain was the angels' tears when I was bad.
The moon seemed to me like a kind face
Through which God looks to see if we are asleep.
Mother told me the clouds were feather beds for the angels
And snowflakes were the dust and feathers coming from Heaven
On cleaning day.
But what I liked best was the big round sun
Which God hung in the sky to help little children to do good.
When I was young I used to think a rainbow came when someone
    in Heaven spilled paint.
And I used to think it rained when Mrs. Thunder Storm woke up
Mrs. Lightning Storm who took his morning shower.
  I thought the sun was a forest fire,
  And the moon a flashlight.
The stars seemed like little silver coins carelessly scattered in the
    sky.

    The homely reality of "Daddy's Vacation" intrigues me.
The full life of farm children is eased by creative writing.
Instead of telling of the flowery side of farming, Helen is a
realist and makes us feel the heavy work of doing the chores.
She was in the sixth grade. Her verse is "bumpy," but some-
how it fits what she has to say.

DADDY'S VACATION

    My Daddy's gone away,
    Don't know just how long he'll stay,
    And when at night from school we come,
    We all pitch in and make things hum.

    Chicks to feed and mash to mix,
    There's horses to water and slop to fix,
    Wood to bring and water to pump,
    Cows to salt, must break the lump.

Supper ready, my! but we're starved,
Cows to milk and practice to do.
And sometimes school lessons yet, too.
Yes, Daddy's gone away,
But gee! We're glad he hasn't gone to stay.

Betty, an eighth grader, seems to be implying in the following poem much which she does not say.

THE WEATHER

The weather is frightful
Like an angry person.
The wind is restless,
Blowing and throwing
The bright white snow.
Children are bold
For they play in the cold.
The weather is a queer thing,
Sometimes angry and furious.
Sometimes playful and smiling.

Phyllis visited a newspaper office. She listened particularly for the sounds and tried to imagine what the machines were saying. Didn't she catch the spirit of a news office well?

THE NEWSPAPER OFFICE

Nimble fingers press the keys
Click, click, click.
To tell a story of the overseas,
Click, click, click.

Workers hurrying, scurrying about,
Stamp, stamp, stamp.
They have a paper to get out,
Stamp, stamp, stamp.

Telephones ringing all the day,
Ting-a-ling-a-ding,
What a noise, I can not stay,
Can't stay, Can't stay, Can't stay.

Have you read Louis Untermeyer's "Peter Putter"?* When I have corrected English papers until I can see nothing but mistakes, I read the following about Peter:

> "While he struggles with his small repairs,
> The large decays eat unconcernedly on."

Few great writers ever pleased their early English teachers. Some of the best ideas came out as undisciplined as a bed of wild flowers. If you see only the mistakes on the paper, you are not yet ready to be a teacher of creative writing. If you see the one good idea or the one colorful phrase on the page, there is hope for you. Take out the old red marking pencil. Underline the good parts of the composition. Now you have some chance of getting some attention paid to your red marks. Remember that we love to look at our achievements; we dislike to look at our mistakes. *Red pencil the achievements.* Pride in one's attainments is a powerful incentive to correct spelling and sentence structure.

I have seen teachers maim with a red pencil writing that was really brilliant in part. True, the rich phrases contained misspelled words, and the sentences were anything but law-abiding. The artist at writing is often not a careful person in regard to details. The very wildness of spirit which runs away with ideas and takes them on untried paths takes them away also from the narrow roads of approved grammar and spelling. Under wise guidance anyone who has anything to say can be helped to say it correctly. The trouble with us teachers is that we spend so many hours helping pupils who have said nothing to say it better. Correctness in regard to detail comes when a writer gets a powerful incentive to write well. Even children want only their best selves on display in the class story book or the school newspaper.

---

* Untermeyer, Louis, *Selected Poems and Parodies.* New York: Harcourt, Brace and Co., 1935, p. 162.

Children need discipline in writing, but the discipline which comes from within is the most effective. Over-discipline may even stifle the creative impulse.

A little fifth grader said to me in my early years of teaching, "There is no use of my trying to use different words in the papers I write for you. The bigger and better they are, the worse I spell them and the more red marks I get. It's cheaper to use little common words that I can spell."

Which do you think is more important, well-written small stuff, or large ideas spelled like something out of this world? There is some hope of improving the second, but of what use are dead sentences beautifully constructed and spelled? Creativity, like flowers, is apt to run wild at first—to be later domesticated through pride in a garden.

Improving the craftsmanship of story writing. Skill in the craftsmanship of story writing develops slowly over a long period of time. As the teacher reads aloud or as the class discusses what it has read, it is possible to point out to children as young as nine or ten years of age such matters relating to the techniques and style of writing as: how the author uses his beginning paragraph to give the flavor of the story, how he builds up the plot, how he delineates character, and how he uses conversation. A child does not appreciate a clock any less after he has found out what makes it tick.

It is possible that too many elementary teachers have been a bit lax in teaching the techniques of writing, since they suddenly dropped the over-teaching of them a number of years ago. We allow children in drawing classes to proceed without patterns, *but we teach them some of the basic principles of drawing which they need to use in their original work.* Many grade youngsters will never improve their stories unless the teachers from Grade Four on make them aware of some of the techniques of craftsmanship. However, there is a great difference between building up awareness and writing one exercise after another to practice the techniques of writing. Awareness is a state of mind which results in a point of view. It develops slowly. It does not come from practice—it comes from observation.

As early as Grade Two a teacher can begin casually pointing out and comparing how stories in the readers and library books begin. In the intermediate grades a cumulative list of different ways of starting stories may be kept on a little-used blackboard throughout the year.

The following list was gathered by a seventh-grade class from observing the techniques used by the different authors whose stories they had read:

HOW STORIES BEGIN

1. With conversation to set the stage for action.
2. With the end of the story; then going back to the beginning.
3. With the middle of the story; then to the actual beginning.
4. A characterization of the chief character or characters.
5. A summary paragraph to tell the point of the story.
6. With description.
7. With the time or place or circumstances.
8. With telling the story according to time sequence.
9. With a question.
10. With just enough of the present action to catch the interest, and then back-tracking to the first of the story.
11. With the background for the action.

An observation of this sort is more effective than working with individual children every time the class writes a story. Reading aloud an interesting beginning that a child has made and commenting on it will help to change the usual "Once upon a time" to a more effective beginning.

Finding out in how many ways characterizations can be made is another interesting class project. In the sixth, seventh, or eighth grade, look throughout the year for examples of character delineation. For instance, in how many different ways can we say that a man is lazy? If we always said it in the same way, stories would be dull. Can you add any to the following list?

1. Simple statement of fact—Bob's lazy.
2. Describing how he does things.
3. Telling an episode to prove the point.
4. Telling of how little of his work is done.
5. Comparing him with other lazy persons or slow things.
6. Using synonyms of the word.
7. Telling what he is not.
8. Repeating his own characterization of himself.
9. Repeating what others say of him.

Unless such an exercise is a matter of observation over a period of time, the results will not be very effective in giving children new techniques in writing. After such an observation has been going on for some time, an exercise such as that just described can be given as an English assignment. If a number of characterizations are used, the results are more interesting. Characteristics that could be used by the different class members are: proud, foolish, wise, honest, hardworking, vain, and selfish.

One class that I visited had observed the techniques of description through one whole year. Needless to say, the class members were better writers at the end of the year. In writing, it is wise to know how master writers handle techniques. If you are lucky, once in several years one of your own pupils may employ an entirely new writing technique. That will be a happy day for you.

All of us need to guard against paying too much attention to techniques and too little attention to the story itself. Keeping the purpose of story telling in mind will serve as a thermostat to control our attitude toward the mechanics. There has always been a war between the humanities and the mechanics, and teachers have not always been the least offenders. Can't we have both, but in their proper proportions?

Evaluating children's assigned stories. All weaknesses in story writing cannot be corrected by class study and observation. Story improvement has gone through every phase from class evaluation, which shriveled the soul of the writer, to minute paper corrections, which shortened the life of the teacher and lessened the story crop. Time is too precious for using poor methods that give poor results. Class exercises and observations will take care of the weaknesses common to most of the class. Personal conference is the only effective way that I know of to handle individual writing difficulties.

Perhaps you have thirty-five assigned stories to deal with. Scan each paper rapidly, making no marks on it. Take a few notes to show what parts of the general class-story-telling are weak. You can work on those points later in class. The next day let the class work at their seats on an assignment in some other subject. Call the children to you, one at a time. Have each read his story to you in a low voice, as you sit beside him. As he reads, read over his shoulder, and the things necessary to talk to him about will renew themselves in your memory. Perhaps his sentences are poor. That is why you had him read his story aloud to you. His reading may tell you what he really meant to say and will tell him what he didn't say.

In five to seven minutes alone with that lad, you can perhaps help him to get a feeling for sentences. If not, perhaps you can give him, and the few others who need it, extra help soon. Sentences may be only one of the dozen things wrong with his story, but forget the rest. *Help him with one thing each time.* There are no marks of any sort on the paper; so he is not defeated or confused before he begins. *Compliment him, first of all, on anything good about his story before you begin to help him with his weak spot.* In the course of a year, after a number of such conferences, a child cannot help improving in his work. Incidentally, you, the teacher, have been saved much home-work, the child's work has not been publicly evaluated, you have been given some good leads to work on with the class, and there has been no loss of time or nerves, since the other children were busy at another assignment.

A few teachers may think that such a procedure could not be carried on in a room of forty pupils because it is time-consuming. May I suggest that you try it three times and note the results before you decide that it does not pay? I know of no other way that pays at all. I have watched too many pupils quietly crumple the papers which I sat up late to decorate with red, and make exactly the same mistakes in their next stories.

Proof-reading stories. The first draft of the best stories is likely to be rather bad. Encourage each child to go back over his story to improve it. Do not require him to copy it in ink until you and he have had your conference. Do not accept a paper for a conference until a child has done the best he can with it. Children, however, appreciate not having to copy and recopy their stories. It makes them hate to write. Copying a story for a real purpose, such as the class story book, is another matter. Children do not like to go through useless motions any better than we do. Listen to yourself at summer school some time when the teacher has made a useless assignment.

If teachers will decide which efforts give good results, they can save themselves and the children much work.

Evaluating voluntary stories. Voluntary stories should not be evaluated unless the writer asks that they be. They were written for enjoyment and should be read for that purpose. However, every one of these stories should be read and commented on to the child who wrote it. The comments should be appreciative and honest, but in most cases should be of a general, rather than a critical, nature. Such comments as these are typical:

> I read your story. I liked it. You like to write, don't you?
>
> Is that a true story, Margaret? I thought it sounded true.
>
> Keep up the writing, Joe. I can tell that you enjoy writing. I'm glad to get it.
>
> I liked best the sentence in your story, Henry, in which you described the horse. That was a good sentence.

A few voluntary stories, however, deserve personal conferences—those that are outstanding, those that show marked improvement, and those that are far below the level of the writer's ability. Outstanding stories will draw comments that help the writer to acquire pride in his work and a desire to improve his techniques. The proper kind of conference will spur him on to more and better writing. A conference about a voluntary story that shows improvement will praise present accomplishments and lead to greater onces. A few kindly words to tell a child that his story was not nearly so good as his usual ones may help to keep him from sinking into mediocrity.

If a teacher is truly interested in the writing of every child, she can draw a nice distinction between being critical and being helpful; between being a "fuss-budget" and having a sense of values. The only way is to test the effectiveness of your results—which results must take into consideration the wear and tear on both teacher and pupils as well as the ability of the writers. If a teacher will remember that she can never teach all the children of all the people to write well, she might relax and enjoy herself while she helps children to get better at story writing.

Thumbnail comments on children's stories. The following stories and my comments should be of interest.

ONCE UPON A COLD WINTER MORN

Silence thunders throughout the household. Outside the black shroud of night moves slowly onward. Lazy bits of cotton float downward....downward. Oh, so silently, so hushed and gently, they land to form a soft white blanket over all.

Outlined faintly against the house....a thermometer....in which the silver substance mercury huddles close....for warmth. Far off....a flowing tone....a bell. Once....twice....three.... four....five. Five o'clock. Five o'clock....on a cold winter morn. Oh, so very cold....so hushed....so quiet....so still. So very still.

Inside the house....a bedroom. Cold....and dark. Ah! The bed. What is this we find? A blanket-hoarder? Six of them.... and a quilt, one on top of another. Inside....rather, down, under,....a shape....a form....of a person. 'Tis I, to be sure. But, oh! such an expression! I look as if I were having a nightmare!....and, from the expression, was just thrusting a shiny steel knife into Mr. Hirohito!

(*The run of thought, causing such an odd expression, is of course on the subject of getting up.*)

Must....be near....morning....have to get up....I spose ....terrible alarm clock!....Why do great men....have to.... waste their time....on such things? Ha! Alarm clocks! They alarm you enough....goodness knows....wake up in the middle of the....night,....an' see its face....all glowing an eerie green from that....phos....phorescent. Nearly scares one....to death ....and,....as if that wasn't enough....the fantz-mi-gastic bundle o'wheels wakes you out of a sound sleep at a simply terrible time of night....by clangin' and bangin' an' yellin' its head off!

Then, last Monday, the great genius's conception went A.W.O.L.; and it didn't manage to fall off the table and dent itself....waking me up....until arithmetic class was over.... missed a test, though! (coincidence of a little incident)

What a nice, handy little noise-maker to have. Grrrrrrr....I'll fix that thing!

A vague picture enters my mind. I am standing behind the table on which the alarm clock always sits....a good, generously-sized sledge hammer raised for a blow! The sledge hammer starts downward....downward!

"Rrrrrrr-Grrrrrrr! Clatter-clatter-clank-clatter-clunk! Rrrrrr! Grrrrr! Bang—Bang—Bang!!" The alarm clock is yellin' its head off....7:15 and another day.

Richard is a great talking point for assigned stories. He rarely writes except for assignments, but, being only in the seventh grade, he has great talent and imagery.

Children's stories speak eloquently of what is troubling them. They point the way for the teacher to know when to be most understanding. These are from grade 5.

THE GIANT

Did you ever look out of the school window and see a whole block being crushed by a huge foot? I did. This is how it happened. One day in school I heard a cracking thunder. I quickly looked out of the window. I saw a huge foot that covered a whole block. I looked up in the sky and there was a huge giant. I thought it was a hundred feet tall. The giant was crushing the whole town. He was just about to step on our school when it started to rain. The giant seemed frightened. He quickly turned around and ran as fast as he could out of town. We were never bothered by the giant again.

TROUBLE

We are always in trouble breaking windows with the baseball. When we paint, we paint our faces. Our mother does not know who we are. When we look at books, we rip the good pages. When we climb trees, the policeman comes after us. Then our mother makes us stay in the house. It is trouble, trouble, trouble!

First-grade and second-grade children like to make up stories together without the teacher entering in in any way. Miss A.... had some pictures on the bulletin board, and this is one result written by two little girls. Notice the typically childish ending.

(TAKEN FROM A PICTURE)

One day a mother bear went swimming. The little bears wanted to swim too. But Mother Bear said, "Oh, no, you are too little. You sit on a rock and watch me. I will show you how when you are big enough."

But one little bear did not want to mind his mother, oh, no, he did not want to mind his mother! When his mother wasn't watching he stepped in and took a swim and stepped out.

And Mother Bear looked at him and his hair was a mess. She said, "Did you obey my orders?" And the little bear said, "No, mother, I didn't obey your orders."

The mother said, "I'll not take you with me again." Then they all went home.

Is the better bitter? Now is the time for every teacher of writing to hold a personal inventory:

> Have my students improved as people through their creative writing?
>
> Has Jim, who can't write, improved sufficiently to have paid for the midnight oil spent on him? Have I made him want to write or have I caused him to hate writing?
>
> Have I helped Mary, who really can write, to refine and improve her writing?
>
> Have I spent so much time on details that I have neglected the large "decays"?
>
> Have I lost my youth and personality chasing A.W.O.L. commas?
>
> Is the better bitter?

Chapter VI

"I Am Fine and Hope You Are the Same"

Letters have made friends—And befriended them;

Letters have broken hearts—And have mended them;

Letters have made promises—And pretended them;

Letters have placated kings—And offended them;

Letters have started wars—And have ended them.

Watch your letters; Lay not your hearts bare

For others to tramp on,

A letter is dynamite—With a three-cent stamp on.

Chapter VI

"I Am Fine and Hope You Are the Same"

T IS *"Read* Letter Day" at Shady Brook School. On the second Friday of each month the English block after the last recess is devoted to letter writing and the reading aloud of interesting excerpts from letters received by the children during the month. The teacher at Shady Brook rural school, realizing how interested children are in receiving letters in the mail, decided to capitalize on that interest to improve the written English of her pupils. Accordingly, "Read Letter Day" was instituted.

Because school time is being used, the letters must be planned before they are written and must be read silently by the teacher before they are sent. The teacher does very little censoring or changing letter content, but she does a great deal toward helping with the spelling. She is of the most help to the first-grade youngsters, of course. Each child places his personal spelling pad on the right-hand side of his desk. The teacher writes any words that the children request on these pads. These words are used as individual spelling lists for the next week.

A thorough study of correct letter forms was made before the project was begun. The children study the letters they receive and discuss together what makes them interesting. The project has proved to be an interesting one. The quality and quantity of the children's letters have vastly improved.

Many letter-writing projects fail because too elaborate plans are required from the class. If letter planning is kept very simple, as it is at Shady Brook, it has a greater chance

113

of becoming a lifetime habit. A plan for a letter should be merely a list of news items, such as this one of Jeanne's:

1. Tell about puppies
2. Ask about rheumatism
3. Tell about frog project
4. Thank for the present
5. Tell about summer plans

Before Jeanne planned her letter to her great-grandmother, she re-read the last letter received from her. This helped her to answer any questions that were asked and helped to determine the tone of her letter.

In planning a letter, Jeanne is learning to keep in mind the type of news each person likes to receive. Her great-grandmother lives alone and is eighty years old. She wants to hear homely bits of news of the whole family. On the other hand, if Jeanne were writing to her Cousin Betty, who is a contemporary of hers, she knows Betty will be interested in anything she has to say. Both girls are beginning to be a little self-conscious about the boys. They will be going to high school next fall. Jeanne is writing a letter today to her brother who is attending college. She will use the same outline for him as for her great-grandmother, but will leave off items 2 and 4 in her letter to him and possibly substitute one other.

Before "Read Letter Day" started at Shady Brook, Jeanne began most of her letters with "How are you? I am fine." In discussing how to make letters more interesting, the children and teacher decided that beginning all letters with the same words was a monotonous thing to do. In fact, Miss . . . . told them that as far back as Roman times letters began in almost that same way: "I am well. If you are well, it is well." Only of course this was said in Latin. Jeanne says that she never starts to write a letter without giggling to herself about "hoop skirt" beginnings and such statements as "I must close now as I have run out of news," or "I must get supper now." No apology is needed for closing a letter when the news is finished. An apology is needed more for continuing a letter after it is finished.

Another chart used on writing days is headed, *The Test of a Good Letter*, and it lists these questions:

1. Does your letter sound like talking?
2. Does it tell the person what he wants to know?
3. Is it interesting?
4. Would you like to receive it yourself?
5. Is it written well?

The Shady Brook children have decided that the folks whose letters sound like talking are the ones whose letters are the most interesting to receive.

Too many elementary teachers judge children's letters by adult standards. Children talk naturally and freely to the people with whom they feel at ease. Help them to write in the same way. I shall never forget a fourth-grade girl who wrote to me, after I had gone away from the city where she lived, and said, "We miss you very much, but we will get over it." How wise the child who, at the age of nine, knows that we eventually get over the things we miss. An adult knows that this statement is true, but would never have said it in a letter. Do not try to make adults of children. Help to make them more observant and more thoughtful children.

The following letters, or parts of letters, were written by elementary children. Notice the sense of humor portrayed in this letter from a fourth-grade girl. Take note too, of how she can make an interesting story from a small happening. *This art is the essence of letter writing*.

Dear ....

Monday something exciting was going on. I don't want to get you excited, but we were getting a new president, OK, not of the United States, of course, but of the Good Readers Club. Katherine was elected president, Nancy is treasurer, Judy is secretary.

Last night I was playing with my doll buggy. The cat sat there watching me. Mamma called me to come and eat. While I was eating, something strange happened. I looked all over for the cat but I couldn't find her. I called outdoors. I called upstairs. I called just everywhere. All of a sudden I heard a meow. Out of the doll buggy came the cat.

> Your friend,
> SALLY

This fifth-grade girl has written a letter as much like herself as if she were talking. She is a quiet child and sees the little things around her. *Letters should sound like talking*.

Dear Miss ....

When we came back to school this morning our room had been changed around. Our desks are slanting now. We had pictures of Lincoln all around. We have the two big chalk drawings made by our children hanging in the back of the room.

There is ice hanging to the aerial. It is swaying back and forth. I think it will fall off soon.

When the teachers gave tea for Miss C...., Miss F.... chose Marilyn A.... and I to help. We had some tea too. I liked it best straight.

I hope you have many friends in .... (and no enemies which I know you will not ever have).

> With my best wishes,
> DOROTHY

This excerpt from a fourth-grade girl's letter shows considerable insight into a mother's care of a sick family. Sharon has five brothers and sisters. *Letters tell us a great deal about children*.

At home we have just got through with the flu and it was hard work on Mother. She was tired out after eighteen hours of work every day. She was the only one at home that did not have it, but she said, "Who would take care of me if I were ill?" And nobody answered so she said, "Don't all answer at once." which startled all of us. I guess we will have to answer next time, "Nobody," for we would not be able to do it.

I hope you are feeling well for we are now.

Well the clock on the wall says, "Tick tock, tick tock, it's time to close," so good-bye for now and Good Luck.

> Sincerely yours,
> SHARON

What a charming beginning Polly has used! She is in fifth grade. Polly has a natural style of writing. _Letters should be natural._

Dear ....

Saturday morning all the trees and bushes were covered with snow. I'm sure that if you would have been here you would have written a poem about it.

The day when the News ladies came Donna went to the teachers and got the bit of news. Miss F. told Donna to get help in writing it over, so Donna asked Marilyn, Dorothy, and myself. We felt like real reporters.

> Best wishes to you,
> POLLY

Donald's rural school visited a near-by log cabin which is furnished with museum pieces. He was so interested that he made pioneer life very real in this letter. He writes especially well for a boy in fourth grade. _Letters should sometimes be a method of reporting._

Dear ....

We wish you a Merry Christmas and a Happy New Year. We miss you.

We are studying about pioneers in Wisconsin. We took a trip to the log cabin. The pioneers heated their house with fire in the fireplace. They cooked their food at the fireplace. Most of the houses had wooden floors but the boards were wide and things often fell down between the cracks. They used candles or lamps to light their homes. The pioneer women spun and wove wool into cloth to make their clothes. We saw the wool carder and spinning wheel they used. They got upstairs through a trap door and stairs that looked like a ladder. Our teacher showed us the trundle bed. The children slept in this bed, which was kept under the big bed in the day time. Their furniture was put together with wooden pegs because they had no nails. We saw the oxen yoke which they put over the oxen's heads like a harness. Their books were very different from ours. The books had few pictures and the print was much smaller.

We are making and doing things the way the pioneers lived. We have made a lovely fireplace. We have made a loom. We are going to make soap when the lye is strong enough. We let water drip through wood ashes and the liquid that drains through is lye. We are going to make butter and cheese for our pioneer party.

Mrs. H.... said you are going to college. We all hope that Santa is real good to you. Come and see us some time.

Your friend,
DONALD

Fourth-grade Roger gives a good description of his baby sister in this portion of his letter:

I have a little sister. She cleans out the drawers and eats all the cookies and dusts the floor and chews on the soap and tears all the books she can get.

Roger's sentence sense is not what it will be, but his baby sense is well developed.

Another child in the third grade writes of his sister.

Our baby sleeps and sleeps, she drinks and drinks. She puts on shoes and takes them off all day.

An eighth-grade boy has made a story of a soldier's letter. He has also very effectively characterized one of his friends. Both of these boys are fine writers.

FIRST RAID

I guess perhaps you don't know Donald. Very few people do. You see, he's quiet and doesn't take part in much of the fun in our neighborhood but when there's a job to be done, he's right there to help. Well, I'll start from the beginning.

Donald enlisted in the air force last January, just after war was declared. After a few months training with the latest planes he was sent to the Philippines. I got a letter from him the other day telling me what happened after he got there. This is what he said:

"I arrived at 6:00 o'clock Monday morning, all the boys are happy and joking but from the first I knew we weren't here for our health, and I was right. The following week we were eating dinner when the dispatch messenger came running in saying enemy planes were headed this way. Well, we didn't wait for any more. It was every man for his plane. By the time we got our helmets and coats on, the mechanics had our ships warming smoothly. Just before climbing in, the flight leader said, 'Don't quit until the finish.' I climbed into my Republic (called Jenny) and gave her the gun. She rose like an eagle never fearing anything.

"Then we sighted the enemy and climbed for altitude. Just before going into battle I heard the C.O. beller, 'Go get em boys.' Well, we got em.

"There were sixteen bombers guarded by twenty-five fighters, so you see it wasn't an easy match to our twelve. The squadron nosed for the middle bomber and was followed by the rest of us to sweep at the fighters. I picked out one black plane and dove for its tail, but he didn't wait for that, he looped and cut at my cock pit. The fire from his guns broke the glass in the rear cock pit, but one of my buddies cut him short and sent him to the ground in flames. That was one for our side. But that same fellow that helped me went down a few minutes later. All together I got five planes and helped them down a bomber. While the other boys pumped lead into eight others. After the second bomber getting shot down, the rest turned tail and fled. After returning to our base we counted the missing. All in all there were four planes missing, but those fellows didn't die in vain because they were defending America.

"I have been in many dog fights now. But many others never came back, but I know they wanted to go the way they did, fighting."

When letters should be written. Some classes in school write letters to the children in the next room. It is well all through the elementary grades to practice the little niceties of living in real situations if possible. One schoolroom has this motto on the wall: "If you can't say it, write it." This terse statement summarizes well when to write notes and when to talk. Ninety-five per cent of our daily communication is oral, and only five per cent is written. It is real living, therefore, to talk our messages when we have the opportunity and to write them when we must.

One teacher has said it this way: "Oh never think a letter or a gift can take the place of a few kind words said warmly—face to face."

There are many opportunities in school to write group letters or individual letters to a person in the community. The teacher who capitalizes on these opportunities for note writing from kindergarten on will have helped children to form the habit of writing.

The sick need letters, and the alert teacher will see that they are written. In small communities not only sick children, but convalescent adults who live near the school, will be glad to receive the children's uncorrected and unexpurgated letters.

Notes of condolence are the messages which even the adults avoid if they can. An adult who has suffered a bereavement needs letters from friends—letters that say very little, if anything at all, about the bereavement. A warm letter telling your friend that you are thinking about him is worth a dozen commercial cards bought at the store.

When bereavements come to the people beloved by the school or to your individual pupils, encourage note writing to the bereaved family. Thoughtfulness should begin at home, but many children will never learn to be thoughtful unless their teachers help them to be.

People need notes when they are in trouble, but they also need them when joy or advancement has come their way. To tell a friend you are glad he has had success is to double his enjoyment of that success.

I know a few people who write little notes to accompany clippings they think will please people with hobbies or special interests. I have received a few such notes myself and know how heart-warming they can be. A teacher who can help children to be thoughtful of others has really helped to educate her pupils.

School is the place where children learn to write thank-you notes within a week after they have been entertained or have received gifts. Few people would mind writing such notes if they only knew what to say. A letter-writing school will teach them what to say. A letter-writing day each week or two will provide the time for each child's letters.

I have often wondered what a school-board member or a school superintendent would say if he received letters from school children in appreciation of a piece of new equipment or new books. If I am not mistaken, it would pave the way for many further gifts. Appreciation is all too rare a quality.

Letter exchanges. The Junior Red Cross Magazine and other school papers in normal times carry lists of schools, both in the United States and in foreign lands, the children of which wish to exchange letters with children of other schools. Such pen pals not only cement friendships among nations, but give children a kinship with children in other lands. I know of two young ladies who for ten years have been corresponding with two girls in New Zealand and in England. The other members of the family sometimes include letters to these girls, and real friendships have grown up across the waters.

The following is a letter sent by an English child after receiving a Junior Red Cross gift box. The last of the letter was lost, but the major part of it is included here. The English children found the name of the school under a label that had fallen off in transit. The school children who received the letter certainly feel close to England these days. (How strange and how unreasonable it is that most of our loves and hates of nationalities are based on one good or bad contact with that nationality in our formative years.)

24 Rowan Ave.
High Wycombe
Bucks
22-3-44

Dear Friends,

I thought that I would like to write and tell you what a lovely party was given here in England by the American Red Cross, and how I thank you for the lovely presents which were sent over by you, to give to the children.

First it was for children of 6 to 14 years whose father is in the forces, or wounded, missing, or has died in this war. My daddy joined up 4 yrs. ago last January. I have 3 sisters, ages 17, 15 yrs., and 19 months. My age is 12 yrs. We also have two evacuee children living with us for 18 months now.

Now for news of the party, etc. We all had to be there at the school room at 2:30. Lots of children came. We had games, dancing, and a lovely tea, lots of cakes, sandwiches, and lemonade to drink. After tea we were entertained by the American soldiers and Red Cross. On the stage was piled high gift boxes, which were given out to us as our names were called. I found your address under a stick-over label and want to write and thank you for them, they were lovely things. Mine contained powder compact, flannel and soap, little handbag in white which I treasure, box crayons, note-book, two white hair slides and a brooch which is in red and white, says In the Army. So I can wear it on my coat as my daddy is in the army too. I do hope you won't mind me writing and also will you write to me as I would love a pen friend from America. Also my sisters Beryl 17, and Dorothy 15 yrs., would like a pen friend to write too. Once again I thank you for all you did........(and this last sentence is gone.)

Letters to make school work real. The radio has been a boon to rural and village schools. It opens the door of imagination and another teacher walks in. "The Story Lady" over a Wisconsin radio asked the boys and girls to pretend that they were their own pets. She asked the pets to write to her telling how their owners cared for them.

These three letters came from a rural school where almost all the children were very poor. Their teacher gave them such a hunger for education that they devoured (and I mean *devoured*) every book they could lay their hands on. Accordingly their written speech as a school was a bit bookish but imaginative and real.

Dear Story Lady,

I am a very jolly rabbit because my keeper gives me delicious dandelion greens. My! but they are refreshing. I also have fresh water every day, too. My master knows how to lift me up as he does it by my loose fur back of my ears and then puts his hand under my lower part. He repaired the pens so weasels or rats can't get me and since he made another one last night, he must be going to get another bunny like me. I hope so. Well, I must get busy because I have ten starving baby rabbits to feed.

Your friend,

Rosie Rabbit (Grade 6)

Dear Story Lady,

I am Curly Cat and I get my name because I curl up by the fireplace. All I do is to eat and sleep for I am very lazy. My mistress likes me more than any other cat in the world. She gives me milk and hamburger to devour which is my favorite treat. To show my appreciation I purr and rub against her. She is kind to me by brushing my hair, petting me, giving me a bath in summer, not kicking me around, and taking me for a walk. I love my mistress, and I surely appreciate my home.

Sincerely yours,
CURLY CAT

Dear Story Book Lady,

I wish my master would feed me a dozen ears of corn. I hoped he would let me get out of here so I can get into his corn field. All of my brothers and sisters are in his potato patch and here I am in this dirty old pen. I wish I could swim in a nice mud puddle. I am getting lonesome, too, and long for some playmates.

Your friend,
MR. GREEDY PIG

Writing to noted people. Letters to famous people should not be stressed much, because children might become a nuisance to a busy notable. However, such letters as the one a rural school wrote to an artist who painted western Indian pictures was a letter of appreciation. The third grade so admired these pictures that they wrote to the artist telling him so. Back came an autographed picture and *a letter from a real artist.* The children just couldn't believe it. Letters of appreciation are always in good taste.

The pupils of an eighth-grade class, having completed a unit on animal stories, decided to write some dog stories of their own. Some of the tales were so well written that they decided to send the best two to a prominent writer of dog stories. They told the author how much they liked his stories and hoped he would like theirs. He did, and he sent them a lovely letter of thanks. This author's kindness may have produced another writer.

Imaginary letters. To go traveling via the book route is always delightful, but the fun is enhanced if one can write letters home from foreign lands. As Dean says, "Maybe you won't believe me, but I really am in Uruguay." And I believe Dean is. Notice how real is his imagery, even to the heading. Most letters of this type will not be so long as Dean's, but this boy likes to write and he is full to the brim of new sights and experiences.

18th of July Street
Montevideo, Uruguay
May 24, 19—

Dear Don,

I suppose you won't believe me, but I am really in Uruguay, the smallest republic of South America. The capital is Montevideo, which is a very modern city. It was founded more than two hundred years ago. Its first buildings were rude shelters made of hide. Now they have skyscrapers and the most beautiful theaters of the world, so you can see what a change has been made since people have become civilized.

The city is about the size of New Orleans, with a population of about three hundred thousand people. Nine-tenths of the exports go through the port of Montevideo. They have beautiful plazas, and the young people come to stay all evening. The streets are wide and very modern and are paved with granite. If you ever come here, you'd better bring your bathing-suit. Don't think you'll get your feet all muddy like you did down to the creek back home. They have bathing houses that you get in and they pull you right into the water. When you get through bathing, they pull you out of the water again. The climate is warm all year around here, never above 72° F. nor below 55° F. There is a good natural rainfall of about 37 inches throughout the year. They have lots of pasture land and raise many cattle and sheep, merino sheep, because they have heavier and better wool. They have some farming and raise wheat, corn, flax, oats, barley, alfalfa, linseed, birdseed, tobacco, and grapes. They have big ranches called "estancias" on which thousands of cattle and sheep graze. The climate is so mild that animals feed in the open all year. Tell Dad and Ma to come out and get a big "estancia" to raise cattle and sheep. They'd make plenty of money soon. "Gauchos" are the sheep and cattle tenders and work quite cheaply. They're like the cowboys of western U.S. The people are very highly educated and are very progressive. They are mostly of European descent and are proud of their ancestry. Like all Latin Americans they are Roman Catholics, but there is religious freedom.

One of the most important cities of Uruguay is Fray Bentos. Many thousands of cattle and sheep are slaughtered here each year. The meat and the fertilizer go to Europe and the hides and wool go to the United States. The schools in the cities are modern and have free lunches for the children. The girls are taught to cook and sew while we boys learn manual training. In some of the rural schools I visited they studied aloud. You just get interested in some book and then some one will probably say, "Simon Bolivar was Dictator of Peru in 1824," and the first thing you know you're reading history instead of fiction. Uruguay had the same thing happen to them as the French people in Acadia (now Nova Scotia) did, but now they have a new capitol and many famous buildings.

The Solis Theater, the largest in the world, is having a good show and I'm going to it. It is a double-feature called "The History and People of Uruguay" and "The Life of a Gaucho." When did you decide to come? Please wire me when you will arrive, so I can make reservations at the hotel. I will take you around Montevideo and show you the new $40,000,000 capitol. In the evening we will go to the Solis Theater and then to one of these South American restaurants. You'll eat food here you've never even heard of before. Say "Hello" to all of my friends back in the U.S.A.

Your Brother,
Dean

Pupils of one rural school spend a year taking a bus trip over the whole United States and writing to their folks once a week. They present a notebook of the letters complete with pictures to their mothers for Mother's Day.

This imaginary letter from an oak tree to a maple was written by a rural child during a unit on Trees. Such an imaginative exercise is fun for imaginative children. It should not be given as a class assignment.

Putman Avenue
Mr. Stone's Yard

Dear Mr. Maple,

I was fifty years old yesterday. I grew from an acorn. I am a big huge tree now. In autumn you know my leaves fall on the ground and help to make good soil. I think I do a little to help Mother Nature, don't you?

Two men are coming to cut me down soon. I wish they would let me live but Mrs. Brown needs fuel to cook with. The men will take me into the yard and split me with an ax.

Come and see me before I die.

Your good neighbor,
MRS. OAK

This same school wrote nature telegrams. I imagine Mother Bobolink must have sighed, when receiving Jimmie's telegram, "These men are never at home when you need them!"

Dear Jimmie Bobolink,
Come home at once. Bill Tom Cat captured our young. Is holding them for ransom.

MOTHER BOBOLINK

Dear Mother,
Coming home today. Stop Tom from eating young.

JIMMIE

A letter is a good letter if it comes from the heart and says what the writer has to say clearly and effectively. Those last two qualities are not found in the letters of many boys and girls *unless they study the techniques of good letter writing.* A good letter contains at one time or other good reporting, description, and story telling, and sometimes includes lines so lovely that they can be called poetry. To write good letters, then, children must learn to do all types of writing well.

Since practically the only type of creative writing done by most adults is letter writing, *children must learn to write letters at school* by beginning in kindergarten or first grade and writing to real people in real situations as often as possible. These real situations can be supplemented by imaginary happenings which call for letters. But never make this assignment: "Tomorrow write a letter." Letters—even more than other writing assignments—must be real; and, for an imaginary situation to be real, a teacher must put a little magic into the assignment.

There is a bit of the mystic and of the magic of the stage in a real teacher.

Words Are New Worlds

COUNTRY TEACHER

She taught us how to understand

The mystery of little living things—

The egg's enigma and the daily miracle of wings.

She taught us how to find within the pages of a book

The answers to the questions

We had brought from field and brook.

Because of her, we'll always long to go

When come the first spring pipings of the birds;

Because of her, all through our lives, we'll know

The color and the majesty of words.

Chapter VII

Words Are New Worlds

EVERY YEAR scientists discover new worlds—new worlds of thought and action. Each new discovery and each new experience brings new words into our language. As our worlds increase, our vocabulary increases.

It is the same in the world of experience. Children learn most of their vocabulary before they come to school. In those first years their experience grows with astonishing rapidity, and their vocabulary grows with it. As the school years advance, children's speaking vocabularies change very little. If children read widely, their understanding vocabularies are rich and full, but their speaking and writing vocabularies are too often lean and inadequate.

How many people do you know who grope for the right word? How many deep thoughts fail of expression because the speaker has no words to express his feelings? In the midst of the richest nation in the world, where the experiences of both average adults and average children are rich and varied, the vocabulary of many is so limited as to be almost illiterate. Why?

Children get their vocabularies at home, on the street, at school, and from books. In many homes, the supply of words on hands is more limited than the supply of groceries on the cupboard shelves. On the street, children learn a rich vocabulary, but not always one suited to polite conversation. Many children do not read books. The only place left to give children an enlarged and enriched vocabulary is the school.

No more useful legacy could a school teacher leave with her school children than to give them a feeling for words— an "insatiable curiosity" about words. Words can be tasted, smelled, heard, felt, seen, and put into action. They help us to understand the world we live in and the people we live with. They help us to know the false. *They help us to say exactly what we mean.* In diplomacy, if we do not have the right words, even our nation is in peril. The wrong word causes us to lose out in business and in the business of living. How many people know half as much about the right word to use as they know about the right costume to wear?

An elementary teacher's vocabulary has a tendency to become sterile because she is constantly with children. She should "talk up" to her children instead of "talking down" to them. Children love new words—the bigger the better—if they do not come too thick and fast. That, I believe, is the trouble with our vocabulary teaching in school. It does not come slowly through use and appreciation. Dictionary work is too often something children must do. Yet I have seen children have so much fun with the modern children's dictionaries that they begged for more.

A teacher cannot give children a feeling for words unless she has it herself. But she can get a feeling as her children get it. The door is open to even the most colorless teacher; but to the colorful, not only is the door open, but the windows are up and the sun is shining through. You may be weak in your arithmetic teaching, be a poor writer, and be a worse musician; but, if you can give your children a feeling for words, you have changed their lives and given them genii which will serve them all their days and lead them into new and strange experiences.

Apparent casualness creates the proper atmosphere in which a feeling for words grows, but a definite program which permeates the whole school day makes a feeling for words a part of a child's being.

Developing taste for words. Taste for words is much like taste in clothes; a few people seem to be born with innate taste, but most people have to acquire it. The teacher is about the only person outside the home who is in a position to help children to acquire a taste for words.

The following suggestions have grown from the seed-bed of experience. You may have tried all of them yourself. They all work under certain conditions. You will have many more to add to the list. These suggestions will be nothing more than devices, however, unless the teacher is of the type who makes her children vocabulary-conscious by opening up to them the "World of Words" as a magic land where we have only to rub our lamps and the genii of imagination appear to do our bidding.

A. As you read a good book or part of a book orally to your children, stop to enjoy colorful phrases and apt words with them. Chuckle together. Do the same thing in reading classes and in social studies classes. Use the new phrases in your own conversation whenever you can.

B. Bring in from your outside reading any choice phrases and words and descriptions which you think the children will enjoy. Soon they will be bringing bits to read to you and to the class. Take time to describe the sky together each morning. Such phases as newly-enameled, tear-washed, blue as a baby's eye, angry-looking, pouty, sagging like a dirty circus tent, wind-tossed, and frowning, will develop real shades of meaning.

C. If a maple tree has grown suddenly gorgeous or a bush in your yard is camouflaged with snow, or if anything happens which especially "sings to the eye," take time during school hours to talk about it, trying together to find adequate words. Make this teaching as subtle and as natural a process as possible. Do not say, "Let us describe this." Instead, get talking about things until the proper words become as natural as the chalk on the tray.

D. Keep a class notebook of excellent words and phrases you find in your reading. Have a page for color words, one for hard words, one for soft words, one for action words, etc. Let only the best get into the book.

E. Keep a class notebook of unusual descriptions you and the children find. Every once in a while, read aloud from the book your class has made.

F. Keep a class notebook of unusual and apt words and phrases that your children use in their writing and talking. Put them on a corner of the bulletin board first before they are written in the book. John wrote this sentence today: "Doris said her baby brother was more trouble than all the baby robins in the nest outside our window." Using this method of praise is *very* effective.

G. Keep a special notebook about trees, containing ways to describe them in all four seasons, in twilight, and at night. Our books are so full of these descriptions, but most girls and boys find themselves without words when they try to tell how trees look.

H. Hunt for words and phrases that establish mood. Using a paragraph from your reading book, find all the expressions that show that this is a pleasure trip, or find all the expressions that tell you it is a gray day both out of doors and in the minds of these children.

I. Blow "word bubbles." After having had a science lesson on bubble blowing, use the same idea to get synonyms. Start each row with a word, such as went, answer, pretty, small, or old. Then, one row at a time, let the children blow their bubbles larger through giving synonyms of each word. The row giving the largest number of synonyms has blown the largest bubble.

J. Pretend that you and your pupils are hiding in a tree along the street, watching hundreds of boys go down the street. From your high vantage point, you can take the sentence "The boy went home," and see dozens of different boys as they go home. For example, there may be the boy with crutches, the fat boy, the boy with the freckles, the sneaky boy, the boy in the checked suit, the tall, thin boy, the boy with sad eyes, the boy with the baby cart, and the boy with the turned-up nose. Another day take those same boys and, one by one, find out from your tree above the crowd just how these boys went home. Each may have gone home differently because of the kind of boy he is—galloped, shuffled along, trailed along, marched erectly; for each boy use a different word instead of *went*. Still another day, picture the kind of home each boy is going to: tumble-down shack, palace, warm comfortable sitting-room, warm supper, etc. This game not only develops the habit of using specific words, but also develops eyes in the heart.

K. Try to write word pictures of the kind of music that comes out of each musical instrument. (This is excellent.)

L. Encourage your pupils and yourself to make definitions of common things, such as bed, chair, chicken, and house. This not only is fun but is excellent training in specifics.

M. Let your children write their own newspaper. They will learn best from actual doing. Praise new vocabulary words.

N. Keep a yearbook of the best poems and stories written by the class. Exchange your book for one from a near-by school.

O. Get children interested in what children of other lands use in place of the expressions we have. Some examples are given in the following list.

Ours	English Children's
wash cloths	wash rags
rubbers and overshoes	boots
rain coats	mackintoshes
breakfast food or cereal	porridge
bedspreads	counterpanes
crackers	biscuits
canned fruit	tinned fruit
faucet	tap
elevator	lift
street car	tram
truck	lorry
subway	underground
gasoline	petrol
movies or moving pictures	cinema

P. Keep choice and usable words and phrases on tiny cards in a box. When there is a minute or two to spare, reach in and take out one or two and let children use them in oral sentences.

Q. Read much poetry to your children. This is excellent ear training. After reading such poems as "The Plaint of the Camel," have fun with phrases such as *crackers to crunch* and *coops are constructed for hens.*

R. Work with rhymes and jingles, not only for better pronunciation, but also for getting a feeling for the music or words.

> "They are yellow, yellow, yellow,
> They are mellow, mellow, mellow,
> Liked by every fellow, fellow, fellow,
> Good yellow, mellow apples."

If you can't find rhymes and jingles that you want, make some up and let the children try their hand at it.

S. Keep a daily diary in your room. First make it together; then a week later let different children write it every day. Try to make it a little better than a mere record. Let it contain feelings, too.

T. Either orally or in writing help your children to
describe: the exact color of the lake, the new
leaves, the song of a robin, the song of a wren, the
song of the wind that howls around the corner at
night, the feeling in the pit of the stomach when
going up in an elevator, and the feeling in the pit
of one's stomach when he is going to be punished.

U. Words such as *good* and *nice* are *tired* words.
Make new workers for their places to describe a
cake, a man, a baby, a party, bath salts, fudge, and
similar things.

V. Get children to notice new words and phrases that
were either little used or unknown before the war
—such words and expressions as communique, establish a beachhead, and jeep. Make lists of them
and add to the lists all year.

W. Get children interested in the foreign languages
from which our words came. Let them give radio
talks about the origin of such words as manufac-
ture (which means to make by hand), and tell how
the meaning has changed. Let them find out from
the dictionary where such words as these came
from:

radius	plaza
banana	sachet
kindergarten	forum
sabotage	kobold
meringue	camouflage
mosquito	memorandum

X. Describe the characteristics of a person or animal
through telling a story about him. Instead of saying, "Our baby is clever," such a story as this will
show how clever she is:

Our great-grandmother uses a long tin ear
trumpet. The other day when we were cleaning
out the kitchen cupboard, the soup ladle was
taken out. Quick as a flash our baby, who is just

beginning to talk, grabbed the ladle, put the little end to her tiny ear, and said, "Grandma."

Y. Change general statements to specific statements. For example, a general statement is:

It is a beautiful Indian Summer day. Specific statements follow:

The air is golden and the haze makes everything look unreal.

The trees stand motionless and the landscape seems to be dreaming.

Z. Have fun with words (a teacher's own words are used).

1. After *Bambi* was read to my second grade I asked the children if they could remember words that the author used to tell how Bambi and the other animals went through the forest, or on the meadow. Here are the words given in a twelve-minute period:

dashed	flashed
rushed	danced
ran	crashed
leaped	bumped
hurried	fell
dodged	stumbled
galloped	limped
jumped	staggered
swam	scattered

We dramatized several to show *shades of meaning,* and also told the difference. We gave sentences or instances from the story to show the meaning. It was hard to go to our next work.

2. Have a space on your board marked "50¢ Words." Write there unusual words that the children bring from their reading and home conversations.

Teaching vocabulary through pictures. Suggestions for using pictures to teach vocabulary follow.

A. Put technicolor in children's writing. Put captions under the pictures you mount and put up in your room. Each *Saturday Evening Post* has at least six suitable pictures for this purpose. We must get children to see mentally as they see visually. Use such captions as these:

> Jack Frost has been making lace again!
>
> These shells cast their stream-lined shadows.
>
> Can you find the exact expression for the look on this boy's face?
>
> Can you find words to describe this sunset?
>
> What name would best fit this kitten?
>
> How would you describe this grandmother's face?
>
> Three silvery geese made a victory sign against the golden moon.
>
> Ripe red strawberries in a bright blue bowl.

Change your pictures often. Don't talk about them. Let them and the captions do the talking.

B. Capitalize on children's love for comic strips. Take *Nancy* and *Napoleon,* for instance, or any other comic strip dealing almost entirely with the children. Talk about the expressions on the faces. Let one child write the episode every time there is an especially good one, paying particular attention to the expressions and the action words. Help your children to see that the caricature artist and maker of comic strips draws as a writer who uses story-telling words writes.

C. Do the same thing with the simpler type of cartoon. Study how the writer makes a cartoon of words by using broad splashing terms which tend to over-color.

D. Gather together animal pictures. For a week or two post all the dog pictures. Then have the class think of adjectives to describe each dog and a general noun to compare him with, such as "He's a regular policeman" or "There's something in this face that reminds me of Winston Churchill." Cats and wild creatures, such as deer, make excellent studies, as do collections of faces of old men and women or babies or adolescent youths. Notice, too, how the subject of each picture walks and try to get the right shade of meaning to describe it. Add new words to the children's vocabulary. Use the dictionary together.

E. Use art pictures for appreciation. When using art pictures of a certain type (Madonnas, for instance), put up many similar pictures of Madonnas as well as many ordinary mother-and-baby pictures. Leave the pictures up long enough for them to permeate the atmosphere. Put captions under some of these. A few suggestions are: "Notice this mother's hands." "What are you beginning to notice about Italian babies?" "All babies are much alike until grown-ups teach them what to believe."

After a few years children may really know Madonnas and, what is even better, they may see the Madonna in any mother who has a baby.

F. Teach shades of meaning through mounting pictures of increasing size on deepening shades of colored paper. For instance, paste a large dog on light yellow paper, a *great* dog on a deeper yellow shade, and a mammoth dog on a deep gold shade. Do the same thing with musical instruments, and have the word *reedy* coming out of one, *shrill* from another, and *ear-piercing* from another. *Pretty, handsome* and *beautiful* can be worked out in somewhat the same way. Drum beats of increasingly louder notes will accentuate the increase of proportion. Words that are dramatized become more real to children.

G. Let your children listen to music. Let them hear "The Hungarian Rhapsody," for instance. Let them paint whatever the music says to them. Another day let them write whatever the music says to them. Do not expect good sentences—you will be lucky to get good word pictures.

H. Encourage children to make up meaningful rhymes. In making rhymes, use the vocabulary words learned in social studies classes. Here is a typical one from a sixth-grade girl.

"Did you ever see a Chinese pagoda?
It's piled up high like a lemon soda."

She made a large drawing to illustrate the rhyme.

I. Make a class story from studying magazine-cover pictures. In such studies, take time to write lists of interesting words and phrases which describe the people, animals, or circumstances in the story and which the pupils may want to use in their own stories.

J. Mount pictures of food for description. Suitable items are a fresh apple pie, a steaming meat dish, and a cool salad. Get the children to tell what the meringue on the pie looks like, how the meat dish smells, etc. The idea behind this, of course, is to furnish ideas and words for every sight that meets the eye.

Dictionary drills and word games. The new simplified dictionaries are making it possible to have many delightful dictionary drills, such as these:

A. Ask Mr. Webster. Write the word *sombrero* on the board. Let each child open his dictionary after you have made this oral statement: "If you had a *sombrero,* would you eat it or wear it? Ask Mr. Webster." Pupils try to find the word, read the definition, and answer the question. Other suitable questions are:

How is Joe E. Brown like a ewer?

John said he heard a ladybird singing in the tree. Shall we believe John?

"You're a regular *dolt,*" said Mrs. Brown to her husband. Was she complimenting him?

B. Clothing store (finding the words that fit). Write *strives* and *tries* on the board. Ask orally, "Which works harder, a man who *strives* to succeed or a man who *tries* to succeed?"

Other suitable questions are:

Which is fatter, a *fat* man or an *obese* man?

Which is higher praise, to say that a pie is *good* or to say that it is *delicious?*

Which is more cruel, to *ridicule* a man or to *laugh* at him?

This game is played in the same way as "Ask Mr. Webster," but it is necessary to look up two words before the evaluation is made.

C. Blood hound (tracking down words). The class together looks up the word *gewgaw.* They find *plaything* as one meaning. Together they look up *plaything.* There they find *toy.* Together they look up *toy.* There they find *trinket.* Upon looking up *trinket,* they find *ornament.* They look up *ornament* and find *decoration.* As the class comes to each word, they discuss the shade of meaning and together notice that the final word isn't what they were looking for at all.

D. Words with many jobs. Keep a special class notebook of words with several meanings. Divide the page of your notebook into at least four equal rectangles. In each rectangle put a sentence showing a different meaning of the word. Always make your diagram on the board first. This is as good a study of semantics as you can get. Even children in the opportunity room love this game. They love to draw the meaning of each word. Write a word, as *man*, on the board. Then write sentences.

First meaning of *man*—a person. Have someone give you a simple sentence, such as "Man has the power to think; animals haven't."

Second meaning of *man*. The baby is a regular man.

Third meaning of *man*. Mr. and Mrs. Brown are man and wife.

Fourth meaning of *man*. My man (servant) will carry up your bags for you.

Fifth meaning of *man*. "Man the boats!" cried the Marine officer.

Another example is the word *fly*. A number of sentences are:

1. Birds *fly*.
2. I will *fly* away from you.
3. Did you see the boat *fly* before the wind?
4. I will *fly* the flag.
5. The catcher caught a *fly*.
6. Her hose caught on the *fly* of the tent.
7. The zipper is sewed on under the *fly*.
8. The *fly* of the flag is only four inches.
9. Kill that *fly*.
10. The trout rose to the *fly*.

E. Hunting for the rest of the family (a great aid to spelling). The name of the family is any such word as *circle*. Look up its meaning and talk about it. Then find all the rest of the family and touch on each. Some of the members are: circlet, circuit, circuitous, circular, circularize, circulate, and circulation. *Catch* and *scribble* and *sign* are other words that are easy to use.

F. Word bee. This is carried on in much the same way as an old-fashioned spelling contest, but each person tells the meaning of the word and then uses it in a sentence so that he shows its meaning. Use lists from spellers and lists from the appendixes of reading texts. Suit the words to your pupils.

G. Verbal tennis. Line up pupils in two rows facing each other. The contestants take turns giving out words, such as *went, angry, pretty,* and *tall.* The first contestant on the opposite side gives a synonym of the given word, the next contestant on the first side gives another synonym, and so on, words being batted back and forth as long as the synonyms hold out. Phrases as well as words are used. The first side to run out of synonyms gets a point against it. The side producing the last synonym starts with the new word and it is given by the one who stands next to the last contestant to furnish a synonym.

H. Radio quiz (after children have become interested in words). Have ready such questions as:

What kind of people are *alert* people?

What is the difference between a *river* and a *rivulet?*

Why is a *weird* sound seldom funny?

Would you rather have a *curious* friend or an *inquisitive* friend? Why?

Conduct as a real radio quiz program.

I. The minister's cat. This word game is funny and fascinating. One person starts by saying, "The minister's cat is an *American* cat (or an *angora* cat, any adjective beginning with *a* being suitable)." The next person must repeat the first adjective and add a new adjective beginning with *b.* Each contestant then provides another adjective until the alphabet is exhausted (and so are the pupils). For example, the minister's cat may be angora, black, careless, deceitful, energetic, fierce, gritty, hostile, etc. A variation of the same game is good for a Washington's birthday game, using adjectives about Washington and putting *not* before inappropriate ones.

J. Word game. Each pupil takes a piece of paper and a pencil. When the teacher says "Begin!" the pupil writes an alphabetical list of words, one for each letter of the alphabet, in proper order (each word must be of two or more syllables). The pupil who gets the list written first, with all words properly spelled, wins the game.

K. "Dogs into Dictionaries" and "Into the Kennel with You" (games taken by permission of Scott, Foresman and Company from *Middle-Grade Activities*, September, 1942). In the first game, the method is as follows: Pretend I've lost a *retriever*, a *greyhound,* a *wolf-hound,* a *dachshund.* Copy these words down as I write them on the board. When I give you the signal, start hunting for my lost dogs. But before you can find them, you have to be pretty sure that you know exactly what they look like. Where are you likely to get the quickest help in matching these words with pictures that show you how these dogs look?" When the children mention the dictionary, begin instruction in finding words in the dictionary—alphabetizing, finding the right part of the dictionary. Explain that knowing how to do these things will help them play the game. "Now we will go on with the game. As you find my dogs, write down after their names the dictionary pages where you found them."

"Here's another 'game' about dogs. See if you don't think 'Into Your Kennel with You' is a good name for it. I will write four pairs of words on the board." (bugbear bulletin; tentative terrific; woebegone woo; spirit spleen). "Where do you suppose I found these words? Why do you think they are in pairs? How could such words be useful to you?" (Here explain the function of the guide words and how to use them.) "Now I will write a list of dogs on the board." (*terrier, bulldog, wolfhound, spitz*). "Which of these dogs belong in the 'bugbear bulletin' kennel? 'Into the Kennel with It,' then, by writing its name in the right blank space." (Bugbear 'bulldog' bulletin). "Do this with the rest of the dogs and guide words until you have every dog in his kennel. When you have finished, check with your dictionary to see if you are right."

"Another dog that is about the size of the brave *Saint Bernard* is the *Newfoundland* dog. *Newfoundland* is also the name of an island. Do you pronounce the word alike in both cases? How can you find out? How many different parts are there in the word *Newfoundland*? What part should be said more strongly when you are using the word to mean a dog? The island? Now say this sentence, pronouncing the word *Newfoundland* correctly both times. 'When I say Newfoundland (nu found' land), I'm talking about a dog. But when I say Newfoundland (nu' fend land), I mean the island." The class is now all set for some profitable work on pronunciation, accent, etc.

L. Learning the alphabet. To find words quickly in a dictionary, one must know the alphabet thoroughly. Put each letter on a card. Mix up the cards. Then see how quickly the pupil can put them together in order.

If you make two sets of cards, two members of the class can race. Or the class can be divided into teams and can have a relay race to see which team wins.

M. Learning to use the dictionary. Write the words *commence, value, kitchen, grain,* and *remain* on the blackboard in a column. Have the children write the numbers from 1 to 5 in a column on a piece of paper. When the signal is given to begin, the children start to find the words in their dictionaries. When one finds the first word, he writes the dictionary page after number 1; then he goes to the second word and does the same. Children want to play this game over and over again.

Category — Bingo

Chapter VIII

Authors—Pint Size

Like a first pair of trousers,

Like new pennies from the mint—

Is to see for the first time

Our own words in print.

Authors—Pint Size

The material on this page and the next one is copied from the transportation section of "Sprouts," the printed creative writing of an elementary school system. Such a publication affords pupils an excellent opportunity to express themselves.

BOATS AND TRAINS AND AIRPLANES

Whoo! Whoo! the wind is coming up.
We'll be caught in the wind.
We'll twirl and whirl
Whoo! the wind is coming up!
—DAVID VERHAGEN
Grade 4 Washington

You hurry with your dinner.
Then down to the boat you march,
And everybody stares at you
With a look that says they wish they could come along.
Up go the sails and off goes the painter
And you are now in what seems a different world.
You enter the lake on a starboard tack.
A sudden gust of wind
Sends you plunging forward into the wide open lake.
The waves are spraying into your face which is covered with
tiny drops of water.

Now you heel a little more.
The skipper yells. "Ready about."
At this command you look to see if your ropes are O.K.
Then comes another swift command, "Hartly."
You feel the swift turn of the boat as it heads into the wind.
Then the boom comes over and you are once more headed for
port.

As you come in you can hear and smell the city.
You let down your sails, make all ropes fast
And start wearily home.

—TOM THOMSEN
Grade 7 Kimberly

The boat says he likes to go swimming,
He says it washes his back,
But my! when he turns over
He gets a nice whack.

—MARJORIE CLARK
Grade 4 Washington

Boats bobbing up and down,
The tide was coming in.
Grey gulls are flying
Over fishing schooners,
Hoping for fish
The fishermen might have thrown in.

—JOHN KALFAHS
Grade 4 Washington

LIGHTNING SAILS

I like most of all the freedom of a boat—
When you are the master and yours is the choice
Of where and how and when you'll go
With whom you'll go and why.

One who has never sailed a boat,
One who has only watched;
Thinks sailing is a lazy-man's love
Completely play and relaxation.

Though sailing isn't all relaxing—in fact it seldom is—
A landlubber thinks, if he had a boat, he would only lie at ease,
And let the fairy breezes blow,
—And steer him on his way!

NOTE.—More of this poem appeared in "Sprouts," but the rest is not printed here.

A wise supervisor once said to a primary teacher, "When in doubt as to how to teach children, watch them quietly as they play together, and learn in which directions they naturally go. Then teach them what you want them to know, in the way that is natural for them to learn; this will save wear and tear on both the pupils and the teacher."

What do elementary school children do when they play without supervision? They play at being someone or something else; they put action into whatever they play; they imitate their elders; they work hardest at a project which is really theirs; they usually grow tired of one activity in a short time and discard it for another, to return to it later. One can hardly observe children without coming to the conclusion that they learn best when they learn naturally, and when they want to learn. What, then, can a teacher do to turn these natural inclinations of children into channels of better writing?

The school newspaper a real writing experience. No one particularly writing experience capitalizes on more of the natural bents of children than does the school newspaper. It is the children's own project—they plan it, and name it, and write it; they correct it, they evaluate it, they type it (if they can), they duplicate it, and they deliver it. The teacher is the adviser and the mentor only. Children of varying abilities are assigned to the various tasks, and shifts in personnel are made several times a year to allow for wider personal development.

A school newspaper capitalizes on the dramatic inclination of children. In writing a school newspaper, children get a chance to play at being reporters and editors. A reporter and an editor will take criticism more objectively than plain Jim Smith, a boy in the fifth grade whose spelling and sentences are not up to par.

A school newspaper gives children the activity they seek. Reporting done on the run is twice as interesting as a composition conceived and written at the ordinary school desk. The meeting with other members of the school staff in committees is stimulating and different from "ordinary ole school."

The school newspaper is published often enough to interest children, but not often enough to bore them; it is a real thing—it goes into homes and advertises the work of the children; it is something of which to be proud and, as such, it must be well done.

Publishing a school newspaper produces good social habits, as well as better habits of writing. It gives a child practice in planning, in working with others, in doing a careful piece of work, in evaluating, and in getting work done on time. These by-products of newspaper writing are more important to democratic living than is the inherent worth of the newspaper itself.

The child with less than ordinary writing ability has more of a chance to earn a place for his articles in the school newspaper than in a purely literary production, such as a poem book or a story book. The work of every child should find a place in the school newspaper. Many school papers contain not only news items and editorials, but poems and stories as well.

Primary children enjoy publishing a large-sized, handwritten newspaper each week. These children are not yet ready to work with duplicating machines, but they are ready to write.

Mrs. D . . . ., a second-grade teacher, had a room of poor spellers one year. After she read Natalie Cole's "Arts in the Classroom," she decided to try a large-sized school newspaper to find out whether such a project would motivate spelling. Since Mrs. D.... had forty pupils in a room where little wall space was available, she changed Miss Cole's idea in this way: The children did not write directly on the news-print; they wrote their news items on ruled manuscript pen-manship paper. After the name of the paper was printed with large wooden type by a second-grade boy, the news sheets were pasted in two columns, newspaper style. The weekly paper contained as many long sheets of newsprint as the news of the week necessitated. Each child wrote as many articles or stories as he wished. No attention was paid to newspaper style. The articles were written in the first person. As a child wrote, he put down the first letter of any word he could not spell and left a blank so that he might receive help later. When possible, he looked up the spelling of a doubtful word in a reading book. All papers had to be checked by the teacher or by a committee before they were pasted in the newspaper.

Mrs. D.... reports that this newspaper helped to get rid of the spelling difficulty in her room. She found that the paper was an outlet to her advanced pupils, since they usually wrote more than one article each week. The manu-script writing in the second grade improved, perhaps because carelessly written manuscript could not be put in the news-paper. Mrs. D.... typed part of the contents of one paper to show the variety of items received.

Weather, March 6-11

It has been very cold all week. We had a snow storm Monday The snow plows were busy. The days have been very brisk and cold. Edythe froze her chin.

The children on Lake Street made snowmen. Some of them looked like real men.

JEAN

My father is working in Texas. He is coming home for Easter. We have a picture of him in his cowboy suit. He has two real guns.

HERBERT

I jumped in the snow. The snow was so deep Jerry had to pull me out.

RONALD

We made a cotton picture in school. We practiced our play yesterday. Miss O . . . read us a story about cotton. I helped my mother shovel sidewalks yesterday. The Kindergarten children played in the gym today. There are twelve more days until spring. The stores here are having a spring opening. This week my mother is knitting me a pair of stockings. I study my lessons every night. It was five above yesterday.

EDWARD

I am glad Easter is coming soon. I have a special reason for being glad this year, because my Grandmother and Grandfather are going to come to our house this Easter and we are always glad to see them and have such a nice time with them.

SANDRA

We had a spring play. I was a butterfly. It was a cold time and a bad time.

LEAH

I went to see my twin cousins. They are both boys. Their names are Jerry and Jimmy. They are two weeks old. They weigh five pounds each. One is big and one is little.

CARL

Monday my aunt had a five pound baby boy at the hospital.

DELOYD

My father got me a kitten. I made a house for my kitten. The kitten was sick.

EARL

I have a good book. I read out of it every night. It has the story of the magpie's nest in it. It has lots of good stories in it.

REUBEN

In Brownie Scouts last week we made waste-paper baskets for the soldier boys in the hospital.

ELLEN

Raymond and his brother came to my home. We made funny masks. We painted them black. We frightened each other with them. The masks had funny ears.

I have a big snowman in my yard. My brother helped make it. It wears a red straw hat. It has a huge nose and a pipe in its mouth. Is it a man or a lady? You guess.

EDYTHE

My uncle and I went down town and I got a new pair of shoes.

NORMA

I have a puppy. Her name is Pal. She gets into lots of mischief.

PATSY

I have a little puppy. His name is Blackie. He is one year old.

MARSHALL

Many single grades publish their own newspapers every month and send them home to the parents. When duplicating facilities are lacking, two copies are sometimes handwritten by the children and sent from family to family. Still other school groups make one copy only and send it from room to room to be read.

The upper-grade class of an elementary school sometimes writes and publishes a paper for the whole school, the reporters acting as news gatherers from each room. In other schools, each room writes its contributions and the upper room merely edits and arranges. There are good points in each of these methods. The first is, of course, a project for one room only, while the second gives a whole building practice in writing and tends to aid school spirit. The first type of paper might well be started by an enthusiastic upper-grade teacher and then be gradually enlarged to include the whole school. These excerpts are taken from an edition of the Sixth Grade Press. These children are the news gatherers for the whole building (note these examples of straight reporting).

SIXTH GRADE CHRISTMAS TREE

The sixth grade has a very nice Christmas tree that almost reaches the ceiling. Richard C.... brought the tree from his home on the farm. The tree has a silver star on the top, red, green and blue waxed paper stars and strings of popcorn. The popcorn was brought by Marion B.... and Karen M..... It has little paper doilies made into angels and other ornaments made of colored paper. The sixth grade has lights on its tree.

MARION K....

STUDY OF COLD PREVENTION IN SCIENCE

In science and health, the sixth grade is studying about colds.

The boys and girls in their health classes started studying just what a cold is. They have suggested topics for further study.

They heard two magazine articles on cold prevention.

On Thurs. Dec. 12, Dr. E.... came and gave a talk on colds. It was very interesting and helpful.

Mrs. B...., our teacher, caught a cold and was in bed a couple of days. (She said she was an example for the beginning of this new unit of study.)

LOIS N....

The following articles must have been preceded by the teaching of the techniques of interview. Notice the attitudes toward others that these children seem to be acquiring.

THE LIBRARY OF THE TRAINING SCHOOL

Miss R.... is the Training School librarian in the afternoon from one to two. She has been a librarian for three years, but this is her first year here.

She likes people that think of others in the library. She says everyone should remember that a library is to study in and read in. In some libraries she said adults talk aloud too, but usually the children talk loudest.

Some new books are: "A City for Lincoln," Tunis; "Adventure Rare and Magical," Fenner; "The Adventure of Jack Ninepins," Averill; "A Little Boat Boy," Bothwell; "Trudy and the Tree House," Coatworth; "Volcanoes New and Old," Colman; and "Then There Were Five," Enright.

The library's only Christmas decoration is a red bowl with evergreens. It is very pretty.

KAREN M....

OUR NEW PRINCIPAL

Mr. G.... was born in Bayfield. He has never lived in our town before. He has passed through the city, however.

He has taught in four different schools. He was principal in one other school besides this school.

Mr. G's pet "peeve" is girls who are not lady-like. He likes girls who are not coarse. He likes a clean attractive girl.

His hobbies are fishing and hunting. He likes to do things on a farm, too.

The thing he likes about the Training School is working with a lot of nice students. He says they are very cooperative. He said he enjoyed teaching one morning in the sixth grade very much.

DONNA RAE M....

The fifth and sixth grade of the T.S. enjoy their new gym teacher very much. Her name is Miss M..... She is from Appleton. She started her teaching here this year.

She is spry and lots of fun and by the looks of things she enjoys children as much as they enjoy her. She's a wonderful sport.

Her eyes sparkle with fun. She's brimming over with vitality.

JEAN E. . . .

All kinds of good writing are found in the school newspaper. This one, from another edition of the same paper, depicts the fine art of explanation—instructions are often given poorly, even by adults.

STUDENT EXPLAINS HOW TO MAKE THE
PUPPET WORK

To make the puppet work put your little finger in the right hand, and your thumb in the left hand.

Put your other fingers in the head.

To make the puppet dance, move your thumb and little finger gracefully.

The accompanying excerpts from a single page of a newspaper, called the Broadcaster and published by a two-room rural school, show two things: first, how a newspaper can serve as a vehicle for creative writing in a social studies unit; second, how it can be used as an exercise in functional English.

LITTLE TOT'S STORIES
(Collected by
Betty Jean K. . . .)

The little tots studied about Sound Communication. They drew pictures about ways that we communicate by sound. Then they wrote stories to match their pictures. These are two of the best stories:

THE QUARRELING
TOWERS
(By Dale H. . . .)

One day, two telegraph towers were talking to each other. One said, "I am bigger than you." Then they began to quarrel. They quarreled and quarreled all day.

When night came the trees said, "Hush, you should be

asleep." "We can not go to sleep. We have work to do," the towers replied.

THE LITTLE ALARM CLOCK

(By Paula B....)

Once there was a little girl and boy. They were sleeping soundly. One night the alarm clock said, "I will have to wake those children up. Otherwise they will be late."

In the morning it rang and rang. But the children did not get up. The last time it rang the little children woke up. When they got to school they were late. After that, the children always minded the alarm clock.

USING ADJECTIVES

We had a class in which we learned how to use adjectives. Adjectives are words that describe a person, place, or thing. We wrote stories, poems, and limericks with these words. Here are two stories using adjectives, right opposite this article.

LIMERICKS

Limericks have five lines. The first two lines are long and both rhyme. The next two are short and both rhyme. The last line is long and goes with the first two. These are some of the limericks we made up:

There was a dog named Rob.
Who was somewhat of a snob.
He stuck up his nose
He curled up his toes
That snob of a dog named Rob.

There was a merry jolly clown
Who was always falling down
He tripped on a rope
And slid down a slope
That silly jolly clown.

(By Phyllis K....)

THE PROTECTOR

(By Jean B....)

One sunny spring day I went for a walk with Dottie, my dog, As I looked up I saw a grand sight. There up ahead lay a mighty protector, a great barrier. My little dog whined as if she realized the strength of the rock before her. What a breath-taking sight this was at the base of the magnificent and beautiful fortress. Yes, this truly was the protector of La Crosse. Dottie began to bark.

"Cheery Chatter" is the name of the sixth-grade Junior High School paper from which the next group of clippings were taken. These children are trying to write "newsy" news.

A DELICIOUS TREAT
(By Frederick Z....)

On Tuesday morning, February 11, the children of the Roosevelt Jr. High School's 6th grade had arithmetic as usual. Mrs. J.... called on Helen R.... to teach the class. Helen was a little bashful at first. But at last she came up in front of the class. She got a little confused, but as soon as she finished talking, she lifted a cake for the class to see. Mrs. J .... had to cut the cake for Helen because she thought the cake would crumble. Everyone in our room got a piece of cake, even Mrs. J.... got a piece. The cake was soon out of sight. I thought that that cake was just about the best cake I had ever tasted. We all liked Helen's cake which she had made all by herself. I'm sure you would have liked to have been there when the cake was passed out.

The school newspaper is a place to bring school problems to general attention.

E-D-I-T-O-R-I-A-L-S
(By Helen R...., Editor-in-Chief)

We have a problem. Our Health Editor has given up his job. Should we appoint a new one or combine both Health and Science? That would give Raymond "Windy" H.... both jobs. We could elect a new one. Nancy C.... would like the job. If anyone has an idea tell me about it.
Thank you.

A school newspaper helps to create and boost school spirit.

THE CHAMPIONS
(By Mary C....)

We have pretty good dodgeball players in our room. The girls won 2 out of 3 games. They really walloped Morgan and

Edison. What's the matter with the boys? Now boys! You shouldn't let the girls beat the boys. Maybe some girls should play on the boys' team. Maybe so. How about it, boys?

Teachers who require some book reports to be written will find that the students enjoy a *Book Report* column in their paper.

MY FRIEND FLICKA
(By Barbara B....)

My Friend Flicka is a story about a brown horse. Flicka means a little girl. I liked this book because it was very exciting. The author was O'Hara. I found it in the school library. When they rounded up Flicka she ran through a barbed wire fence and was motionless for 2 days. Did she die? Read the book and find out.

The child who is interested in new vocabulary words would like the column from which this item was clipped.

DRUPE
(By Sally W....)

I suppose you are wondering what this is about. Most people think of a drupe as a person who doesn't know something someone thinks he should. The kind of a drupe I'm thinking of is a fruit containing one seed covered with a hard covering or a "stone." The pulp is not divided into segments like that of an orange. The fruit is usually covered with a thin skin. Common fruits that are drupes are the olive, plum, cherry, and the peach.

A school newspaper gives children a place in which to print stories and poems that grow out of the study of science.

ORION'S BELT
(By Sally W....)

One day many, many years ago Apollo, the sun god, borrowed Orion's belt to hitch his horses to his chariot. A few years after that four boys had a contest. Their contest was to see who could throw the highest. The first boy's stone went the highest and it stayed in the sky, but the second boy was a weak boy and his stone fell back to the earth. The third and fourth boy's stones each stayed in the sky. Then there came a flash of lightning which hit the stones and changed them to stars. The three stones formed Orion's belt and in this way he obtained another one.

MARS
(By Paul L....)

I took my rocketship up to Mars,
Way up there among the stars.
I found giants big and tall,
But to them I looked small,
All they did was fight and fight,
And that is why I left that night.

NIGHT
(By Donna C....)

The stars in the heaven, the stars in the sky,
The little stars twinkling, and winking away,
Are sending a message to Venus and Mars,
That's why they wink and sway.

The man in the moon though he looks young and gay,
Is really a very old man,
He's chased away bad dreams, brought in the good,
And made little children a sandman.

The night sky is as black as can be,
With little stars peeping and saying to me,
"Why not come up *here* sometime,
And sail away in the Milky Way Sea."

THE EVENING SKY
(By Frederick Z....)

The evening sky
Is made up of stars
And also some planets
Like Venus and Mars.

Most people like
Scientific study
Which is important you know
For everybody.

The sky is like an endless crater
So deep it looks dark blue.
Every time you look up at the sky
A star winks down at you.

(Unlike most children's poems, in this one the last stanza
is the best.)

An interesting outgrowth of the newspaper idea is a
historical newspaper which a history class publishes during
each period of American history studied. The class pretends
that it is transported back to the Revolutionary Period, for
instance, and writes news items, editorials, and advertisements of that day. These articles from *The Athenian News*,
a historical paper written by the sixth grade of an elementary school, show how real these ancient experiences can be
to children.

ULYSSES HAS NOT RETURNED

The great warrior Ulysses has not returned home with his
men from the battle of Troy. We believe that the God Poseidon
is angry with him for we have heard reports that he and his men
blinded Poseidon's son. We believe that Poseidon in his anger
has sent a sea monster to break Ulysses' ships and to eat the men.

Ulysses' wife, Penelope, already has many suitors. She has
promised to wed one of them after she has finished weaving a
robe. But every night she tears out what she has woven during
the day. The suitors have discovered this and are angry. Now she
has promised to wed the man who can hit the target with the
great bow of Ulysses.

JOAN H....
JOYCE R....

TROJAN SPIES

Athens—

Twenty Trojans were caught today. They are believed to be spies. Records prove that all of them were once members of the Trojan army. Five of them will be executed tomorrow. The others will be sold as slaves in the market in the late afternoon of tomorrow.

ATTENTION PEOPLE OF ATHENS

The blind poet, Homer, will recite another of his famous poems, Sunday, when the sun is high. It tells of Ulysses and how he wandered for ten years trying to find his way home.

HESTIA'S COLUMN

Some of our new Greek homes are very attractive. If you were to go down Athens Avenue you would see a beautiful house.

This house is built around a courtyard. All the rooms open out onto the courtyard. In the living room, there is a large altar on which they offer up sacrifices to their Gods. Next to the living room is the banquet room. In the banquet room there are little tables and many couches where men lie while they eat. Some of the rooms even have rugs on the floors.

The bedrooms have beds which have feather pillows and wool blankets on them.

Back of the bedrooms are the store rooms. Back of these rooms are the slave rooms which are poorly furnished.

On the second floor are the women's rooms which they must go to when strange men are in the home.

The historical newspaper is doubly effective because it capitalizes on three of the things children particularly enjoy —imagining, dramatizing, and taking an active part in an interesting project.

One school publishes a Paul Bunyan newspaper each year in the seventh and eighth grades. Ordinary news is rewritten and distorted until each article is a "tall tale" that even the most gullible couldn't possibly believe. The student with an ironic twist to his writing really enjoys contributing stories for this edition, since the utter fantasy of the whole idea gives him an opportunity to find his own style. The more unusual the situation, the easier it is for a writer to venture into a style of writing new to him.

School poetry and story books. It has been suggested elsewhere in this book that the best poems and stories of each child in a room should be collected into a book for parents and friends to read during the year. If such books are given real names and are attractive-looking, they are a powerful motivation for story writing.

Some buildings have a book for the whole school. At the end of the year a committee of children and their teacher select the most excellent stories and poems from their class collections. Surprisingly, these will not be from the best students in most cases. The writing child is not always a good student. These selections are re-written by the students and put into a large book in the principal's office or the school library. Children take a great pride in getting their work into the school collections. Such books can be made even more attractive if the children design original covers and illustrate some of the poems and stories.

Contributions to local newspapers. Some local papers in villages and small cities will give space in week-end editions to children's stories and poems. An entire school paper printed in a local newspaper once each month or each two weeks is a good project not only for a school but also for a newspaper.

Children's magazines have columns for contributions from children. Encourage your writers to send material to these columns. A few magazines have lists of schools the pupils of which wish to exchange poems and stories with children of other schools. Any procedure which will give boys and girls an incentive to write is worth any effort or time a teacher may devote to it. The best teacher, of course, arranges to have the details taken care of by the children themselves.

Once in a while an elementary-school child writes almost a book-length story. "The Squirrel Family" is such a story and is remarkably well done for a child of ten. Jacqueline had just seen "Bambi" on the screen, and the influence of that story is felt considerably throughout the book. Since this is a first draft of the story (at least the first draft to reach the teacher), some of the vocabulary is extraordinary for a ten-year-old. The observations on life will make adults chuckle as they read.

THE SQUIRREL FAMILY

The three children Morty, Dotty and Daisy were born in a dark hollow tree in the northern part of the United States.

The first days of their life were spent in snuggling around their mother.

One day something sharp hit them. It hurt only their eyes but they didn't like it.

Their mother wasn't afraid.

It was only their father.

He looked in very proud and happy.

"How do you like them?" asked Mamma.

"They're fine," said Papa, "but who's who?" he asked quite puzzled.

"Oh you men!" said Mamma.

"Now this one is Morty," said Mamma.

"This one is Dotty, and here is Daisy," Mamma said.

"This one is Morty," said father as he pointed to Dotty. "Here is Dotty," he said as he pointed to Daisy, "and here is Daisy," Father said as he pointed to Morty.

"No, no! You've got them all wrong. But right now you'd better go out and find something for them to eat."

A little while after Father left, in came Aunt Dootameetafa. She walked right in for she never knocked.

"Why good-morning my dear. How are you today? Oh, aren't the children sweet. What are their names."

"Well,"—But that's all Mamma got in for Aunt Dootameetafa was an awful chatterbox.

Just then she remembered her husband.

"Oh, dear!" she said.

"I've forgotten Timothy. Come in Timothy" said Aunt Dootameetafa.

"Look at the children. Aren't they sweet?"

"Ah"—was all Timothy could say for just then Aunt Dootameetafa burst in again.

"You know our children aren't that sweet."

"Oh I'm very sorry my dear but we must be going now. Come along, Timothy," said Aunt Dootameetafa.

She just got out of the door when she poked her head in again.

"Kiss the children goodby for me."

Mamma took a big sigh after Aunt Dootameetafa had left.

"Whew! Children, don't ever grow up to be like your aunt." Just then Papa walked in.

"What you missed!"

"What I missed! Why if I didn't do some quick thinking I would have gotten stuck with her" exclaimed Papa.

Two weeks later the children were much bigger. In fact, they had even gone outside the house.

One day the children were outside when suddenly they all ran in at once.

"Mamma! There's a very bright red animal down there. We don't like him, he's wicked looking," Dotty said in a frightened voice.

"Oh dear," Mamma said.

"It must be the fox. Don't you ever go off this tree if he or his wife is around."

"We won't, Mamma," said Daisy.

"One thing more," Mamma cautioned.

"If you ever see that fox or any other, you must freeze. Those foxes bring no good; and if they ever catch you they'll eat you. You don't ever want that to happen."

"Oh do they eat you?" asked Morty.

"I'm afraid they do" Mamma answered.

"Oh how horrible," Daisy shuddered. "How can people do such things?"

"Yes it is a horrible thing" Mamma said, "But then some people are horrible too."

"Including foxes" Dotty said.

Then Mamma very carefully peeked out of the house.

"He's gone," said Mamma. "At least I don't see him."

Then Papa (who had been quiet) spoke up.

"Let me look out. Look at that bush over there," he said pointing toward a certain bush.

There was something red behind it. Just then it moved.

Mamma and Papa both were sure it was Mr. Fox.

They didn't know it but what they saw was Mrs. Fox.

A little while later the red form moved away.

You see the foxes were playing a little trick. Mrs. Fox was supposed to be seen. Then she would walk off. As soon as she had disappeared from the squirrel's sight she would circle back and hide where the squirrels couldn't possibly see her. Meanwhile Mr. Fox would be hiding nearby.

A little while after the squirrels would see Mrs. Fox go they would permit their children to go off the tree and they themselves might climb down. Then Mr. and Mrs. Fox would jump on the squirrels and have a nice dinner.

When they started their plans they were awfully upset when a noisy robin warned the squirrels.

Then the foxes, very disappointed, sneaked off.

The next morning all the squirrels went visiting.

They stopped at the racoons. They climbed the tree and knocked at the door.

When Virginia Racoon opened the door, she looked quite disappointed, and said "Oh" as if she didn't want to see the squirrels. She tried to smile the best she could but she didn't do a very good job of it.

"What's the matter Virginia?" Mamma asked.

"Were you expecting someone special?"

"No No" said Virginia.

"No one at all."

"I can see it in your eyes Virginia. There's someone coming here that's more important than us" Mamma said.

"Who is it?" Mamma demanded, but in quite a kind way.

"Well," said Virginia quite hesitatingly, and then she blurted it all out.

"It's my husband. You know he's been gone for a year. Well I got word yesterday from a crow that said he saw him just two miles away. He should be getting here this morning. I couldn't sleep last night just thinking about him."

Then there was a knock at the door.

Virginia hastily went to open it; but before she got there the door opened.

"Henry" Virginia shouted.

"Virginia"—Henry shouted.

The squirrel children just looked on and smiled. They had heard all about Virginia's husband Henry.

He once outsmarted three hunters and saved every animal in the woods.

The squirrels then left the racoons to themselves.

The squirrels told the skunks all about Henry's return, the skunks told the deer, the deer told the rabbits, the rabbits told the robins, and robins were regular newspapers so in only a half hour everybody in the forest knew about Henry's return.

Many months later some white things fell down from the sky. At the time, the children were outside. They all ran in at once.

"Mamma," Morty shouted.

"A cloud is falling down."

Mamma looked out the door and said,

"That's not a cloud falling down. That's snow. Snow comes down every winter. It's cold and wet."

"And pretty" said Daisy in admiration.

"Snow means danger for the deer" Mamma went on to say.

"In just two weeks it will be as high as the first limb on this tree."

The children went outside to play in the snow. They liked it.

In two weeks the snow was not only as high as the first limb but it reached as far as the second and third limb.

The children knew fully what danger was now. They had warned the deer several times of hunters. The deer were nice people and were forever thankful to the squirrels.

The winter passed slowly and drearily, but finally all the snow was gone.

Twitterpatting time! That's what Papa called it.

Just two days after Papa told Morty all about twitterpatting, he saw a pretty little female and the pretty little female saw Morty.

"Ahem" said the pretty little female.

Morty stopped dead still. He turned his head around, his eyes opened as far as they would open. Something went click; something else pounded awfully hard and Morty's head started going around in circles.

Morty was twitterpatted!

This young female worked awfully hard on Morty and before he hardly knew what was happening, Jenny had him in front of Parson Squirrel saying his "I dos."

Dotty and Daisy were getting to be quite young ladies now.

One day Dotty came home with a good catch.

He was a very polite young man named Donald.

Two days later Daisy came home followed by a handsome young squirrel named Harry.

They had a double wedding.

The birds sang their sweetest; the deer looked their best; the rabbits had on their finest coats.

The wedding was a very pretty thing.

> JACQUELINE M . . . . (Aged 10)
> Grade Five

Some junior and senior high schools publish their best writings of the year in an annual booklet. If the school has a print shop of its own, the printing can be done at a minimum of expense. There is one danger in a publication of this sort—that the end-product of writing becomes more important than what the writing has done to and for the child. Most children long to see themselves in print—and rightly so. Pride is a powerful drive in the changing of habits and ambitions and lives. But when a publication goes beyond the hand-written or mimeographed stage and is forever caught in the finality of print, the child who is at all sensitive will realize that, since none of his writings are included in the selected list, he is not really good at writing. As soon as he comes to this realization, like many a child who suddenly faces the unreality of Santa Clause, there is no longer real fun for him in writing. It is just as well to delay the printing of children's writing at least until senior high school.

Children's own publications—hand-written or mimeographed—are of the greatest help in the motivation of children's writing. Perhaps this is because they make use of so many natural inclinations of children.

A creative program in your school will constantly challenge and delight you. You will find the atmosphere of your school room gradually growing warmer and more natural. The children will be normal, lovable children, not tense bundles of nerves. Your sense of what is important will change little by little, with your point of view veering to the child's side. In fact, the by-products of creative writing are far more important than the writing itself. Behind the story, the poem, and the letter; behind the clear, concise sentence or the stumbling search for words, is the child and all that he can become. Creative writing is just another way to understand him.

BIBLIOGRAPHY ON CHILDREN'S CREATIVE WRITING

Appy, Nellie, *Pupils Are People*. New York: Appleton-Century Co., 1941.

Arbuthnot, May Hill, *Children and Books*. Chicago: Scott Foresman and Company, 1947.

Cole, Natalie, *Arts in the Classroom*. New York: John Day, 1940.

Conrad, Lawrence H., *Teaching Creative Writing*. New York: D. Appleton-Century Company, 1937.

Department of Elementary School Principals' 20th Yearbook, *Language Arts in the Elementary School*. Washington, D. C.: National Education Association, 1941.

Department of Elementary School Principals' 23rd Yearbook, *Creative Schools*. Washington, D. C.: National Education Association, 1941.

Duff, Annis, *Bequest of Wings*. New York: The Viking Press, 1944.

Ferebee, June, and Others, *They All Want to Write*. Indianapolis, Ind.: Bobbs-Merrill, 1939.

Mearns, Hughes, *Creative Power*. New York: Doubleday-Doran, 1937.

Mearns, Hughes, *Creative Youth*. New York: Doubleday-Doran, 1929.

Mearns, Hughes, *The Creative Adult*. New York: Doubleday-Doran, 1940.

Ragland, Nannie, Comp., *Children Learn to Write*. Chicago: Pamphlet publication No. 7 of the National Council of Teachers of English, 1944.

Witty, Paul A., *Creative Writing Climates. Childhood Education*, XVII, Feb., 1941, p. 253-257.

Witty, Paul A., *Living and Growing in Wholesome Schools*. Washington, D. C.: National Education Association, Sec. I in *Mental Health in the Classroom*, 13th Yearbook, Department of Supervisors and Directors of Instruction, 1940.

Witty, Paul A., *Realms of Gold in Children's Writing. The Elementary English Review*, March, 1945.